Change your perspective--
change your life

Help Yourself!

Carlos Gutiérrez
Our world is getting better
through higher consciousness

Gotham Books

30 N Gould St.
Ste. 20820, Sheridan, WY 82801
https://gothambooksinc.com/

Phone: 1 (307) 464-7800

© 2023 *Carlos Gutiérrez*. All rights reserved.

No part of this book may be reproduced, stored in a retrieval system, or transmitted by any means without the written permission of the author.

Published by Gotham Books (September 21, 2023)

ISBN: 979-8-88775-070-5 (P)
ISBN: 979-8-88775-071-2 (E)

Because of the dynamic nature of the Internet, any web addresses or links contained in this book may have changed since publication and may no longer be valid.

The views expressed in this work are solely those of the author and do not necessarily reflect the views of the publisher, and the publisher hereby disclaims any responsibility for them.

AUTHOR'S NOTE

Help Yourself! is about remembering what it means to be a spiritual being. It is about personal choice. It is my hope that the wisdom within this book will help you to examine and question your old mind's perspective, especially that approach has not been working out for you.

Help Yourself! is for those who have the desire to experience their inner self and evolve spiritually and for those who are already practicing spirituality and want to grow even more. It has been written to serve as a reminder to us of our true spiritual reality and is based on my personal experiences and the inspirations of my multidimensional soul, angelic beings, spiritual guides, and other wonderful light workers.

I know that the world is getting better through higher consciousness and I believe that there are a thousand ways to evolve spiritually. Understanding and honoring your spiritual awareness can help you to grow faster, from your current "human" state of mind to a more evolved spiritual state. Each of us embraces our spiritual path in a unique way. We are each different, magnificent, divine beings, and no one person is better, worse, superior, or inferior to another. We are all one family in this universe!

I assume my soul (my consciousness) chose my parents and selected the place and year into which I was reincarnated and choose my birth order in the family. My soul also attracted particular people into my life so I could pursue my spirituality through my own decisions and most importantly through my spiritual internal experiences.

Help Yourself! expands on portions of my last book, *Our Spiritual Truths*. In this, my newest book, I share important spiritual self-revelations with you in the hope that these insights will deepen your awareness. I am honored that you have chosen to make this book a part of your life. Thank you.

ACKNOWLEDGMENTS

I would like to thank my life coach and best friend Spirit, who resides within my soul, for her continuous inspiration and guidance throughout my life. I am thankful for the spiritual enrichment produced by my past and present transcendental experiences and look forward with heartfelt gratitude to all people who manifest themselves in my future. Thanks, too, to my family, friends, and acquaintances for contributing to this book and for allowing me to be my true spiritual self. My thanks to Rose Winters for her comprehending editing. Finally, thanks to my friends, Kathryn Abdul-Baki, and Adam Whitley for their suggestions and final proofreading.

Most importantly, thanks to every one of you who had the courage to temporarily put your present old mind's perspective aside and read this book. I hope your experience with the spiritual wisdom in these pages will encourage you to join me in co-creating a more evolved society among our families.

FOREWORD

What is life? What is the soul? What is the mind? What are emotions? What is spirituality? What is the universe? Who are we? What are we doing here? And most important of all: What is love?

These are some of the most important spiritual questions we are always pondering. To help co-create the end of the problems in our world and take total control of our lives, we need to answer these questions. Our governments and religious leaders need to reflect on them and thereby spiritualize our educational, social, political, military, economic, and justice systems. If we can answer these questions, we can end our violent behavior, injustice, frustration, suffering, hunger, fear, and darkness, and experience spiritual evolution to bring the magnificent human race together as one family.

If we continue to believe we don't have the answers to these spiritual questions, we will prolong our struggle. If we strive, instead, to understand our spirituality, life will be so much easier. If we understand that these spiritual answers have been within our souls since time immemorial, since the first "Creation," we can change and heal ourselves tomorrow.

Table of Contents

AUTHOR'S NOTE iii
ACKNOWLEDGMENTS v
FOREWORD vi
Introduction ix
Chapter 1 Mastering Our Lives 1
Chapter 2 Life Changes 6
Chapter 3 Our Mind 10
Chapter 4 Our Old Belief System 14
Chapter 5 The Power of Illusions 18
Chapter 6 The Concept of Time 25
Chapter 7 Toxic Lies, Doubt, and Trust 28
Chapter 8 Our Spiritual Emotions 34
Chapter 9 Expressing Our Internal Love 42
Chapter 10 Love Relationships 49
Chapter 11 The Miracle of Sex 58
Chapter 12 Friendship 63
Chapter 13 Similarities Attract 65
Chapter 14 The Human Family 68
Chapter 15 Our Divine and Eternal Soul 76
Chapter 16 The Power of Meditation 81
Chapter 17 Beingness for Empowerment 84

Chapter 18 Spiritual Inspirations 90

Chapter 19 Our Amazing Spiritual Energy Centers. 94

Chapter 20 The Wisdom of Dreams....................... 103

Chapter 21 Spiritual Healing.................................. 108

Chapter 22 Healing Experiences............................ 114

Chapter 23 The New Holistic Life Coach............... 118

Chapter 24 Your Health 120

Chapter 25 Our Inevitable Transition and Reincarnation 124

Chapter 26 Our Conventional Music 132

Chapter 27 Some of My Spiritual Revelations and Experiences 136

Chapter 28 The Physical Body................................ 150

Chapter 29 Our Powerful Brain 160

Spiritual Definitions... 164

Soul Mantra for the Mind....................................... 169

Conclusion 170

Introduction

Throughout my life, I remembered being a spiritual messenger from past lives, and now I am repeating similar goals in this world to serve others. After a lifetime of observing others' mental, physical, and spiritual characteristics with the help of my family, students, friends, teachers, and acquaintances, my many intuitive observations have been validated. Now, after several decades of spiritual awareness and research, I have shared in this book my insights from observing these behaviors.

We have returned to this world to recreate ourselves as spiritual beings. Until now, we had forgotten our spiritual true essence, had forgotten that indeed, this universe where we come to enjoy ourselves while evolving into higher consciousness and becoming masters of the universe.

This is your journey. In this spiritual quest, there is inevitably a happy ending, regardless of the conditions you had, now have, or ever will have. Remember, life is an endless game, which no one can ever lose.

There is no right or wrong; there is simply what works for you through your own awareness, decisions, and actions. You can become unconditionally loving with everyone and everything; this is the grandest aspect of life and experience. Until now, you have been looking everywhere for answers to evolve in consciousness and become one with Spirit in this world. Now you have found what you have been looking for. Practicing the truths in this book will set you free from all your mental suffering (lower consciousness), physical pain, illusions, and feelings of separation. You will be united with everyone in this world through your spiritual evolution—now and forever.

Throughout my life, my soul has attracted meaningful friends and acquaintances to me. It has encouraged me to pursue spiritual advancement by becoming aware of, and remembering, the inner spiritual knowledge I've brought into this world. The wisdom in this book is global and universal, present in our souls from the day we materialize in this physical life. I have used this wisdom to change my own mind and to enhance my spiritual path. It has worked for me; it will work for you too.

If you are reading Help Yourself! you have been drawn to it by your higher self (soul), and the time is right to allow the wisdom in this book to heighten your spiritual growth. It is important to know that there are no accidents, coincidences, victims, or destinies in life, but creators and co-creators. Every thought and action of your mind, body, and soul is an act of self-definition, which generates consequences based on the level of your spiritual awareness or unawareness.

Reading this book and practicing its spiritual truths will help you evolve into a higher consciousness. I hope you will practice the wisdom from your favorite chapters, experience your consciousness, and thereby manifest your highest purpose in life.

Chapter 1

Mastering Our Lives

Mastering your life is the fundamental key to opening the door to a more successful you. Spiritual mastery, financial stability, and social harmony are all desirable forms of success.

Living your life "unconsciously" may produce misperceptions, such as a belief in luck, accidents, coincidences, destiny, or the belief that a so-called higher power is responsible for your circumstances. Living your life consciously, on the other hand, produces awareness and allows you to make wise choices and co-create positive experiences with others. Such actions will help you to master your life.

(Note, remember that this higher consciousness the world is releasing more than ever doesn't mean that this energy will come to you, and you will change. We need to choose this energy to evolve together, experience oneness, and help others).

Attaining spiritual awareness or mastering your life can lead you to become the creator of your own life path and take responsibility for what unfolds for you each day. As the master of your own life, you will be empowered to meet every challenge in order to evolve in consciousness. For example, if you believe you are unworthy, imperfect, or untrustworthy, that is the kind of person you may become, because your belief becomes your truth and will manifest. But if you believe you are confident, trustworthy, and deserving, you will be on the road to becoming that person.

If your life has been a challenge, it may be because you have been repressing your spirituality by blindly following what your traditions, upbringing, education, and institutions have taught you. If you continue to do this, you will continue to face challenges and experience mental, physical, and emotional separation from others. If you have the desire to master your life, then you need to put aside your old mind's perspective and develop new spiritual perspectives to change and master your life.

Don't confuse your purpose in life with your personal talents. The purpose of life and why you are here is to express your love and compassion to others and to keep spiritually evolving to master your life. However, your personal talents such as being a writer, singer, dancer, athlete, businessperson, medical professional, etc. are the experiences you bring from your previous lives. Follow your excitement or your passion in life while you are spiritually evolving, then you can truly and enjoy life to the fullest.

I have mastered my life by practicing my spiritual perspectives along with developing my careers as a dance professional, life coach, and spiritual healer. My spiritual perspectives are still evolving and changing into deeper wisdom, so I can live my life with little stress, worries, and as healthy as possible.

I would like to share some important spiritual perspectives on how to master your life:

Life is a process of remembering that you are love, compassion, peace, joy, and wisdom so you can evolve through this higher awareness.

∞

Life is a fun game (spiritually evolving), so you can enjoy yourself moving up. Enjoyment opens your mind so your soul can bring you deep awareness and insightful experiences. All life experiences (positive and negative) lead to spiritual growth and mastery of your life.

∞

Living your life spiritually will develop your incredible intuition and creativity. You will be healthier and happier, and you will have fewer challenges and worries. Nothing chooses you or comes to you in life by accident. Everything comes to you because you have co-created with others or are attracted to it as an opportunity to evolve through positive and negative experiences.

∞

The more spiritually evolved you become, the more protected from danger you are going to be through your soul's higher consciousness. Your soul's higher consciousness most of the time will create positive experiences.

∞

Be aware that life is a process of recreating and materializing (in this physical and spiritual dimension) by the Spirit (our Creator). Every element of our physical world is mirrored in the spiritual world—the choices and possibilities of experience are endless.

∞

Life in this spiritual and physical universe is energy, which is an internal experience that exists in your soul, and it is mindless. Life is always in motion, moving up—not down, moving forward—not backward. Look forward to moving forward spiritually so you can enjoy life.

∞

Life, which has positive and negative forces, is not a school in which you come to pay back karmic lessons from past lives. Life is spiritual evolution through the choices you make while you are in this physical form.

∞

Allowing yourself to understand love (the highest energy in the universe), you can experience through your soul, mind, and body the oneness, compassion, freedom, joy, wisdom, and peace in yourself and in everyone else in this world.

∞

Never give up your personal freedom to others. Freedom is power from within that can help you follow your own spiritual wisdom and improve your self-identity and self- confidence.

∞

A spiritual life can lead you toward self-realization. It allows you to disregard other people's conventional old mind's perspectives. Through your soul, you can create your own perspectives about life.

∞

Live your life by choice (being aware). Make conscious decisions and take conscious actions. If you live life by chance or by coincidence (unawareness), you are allowing your past experiences to create your present experiences at the subconscious level. It is important to remember that you are not your past, but your life is always in front of you.

Many of us are living life 90% of the time at the subconscious level (routines) which makes it harder to expand our minds and reach higher consciousness to bring balance in our lives. We have become too comfortable being in the box of our mental, emotional, and spiritual limitations. However, it is never too late to grow spiritually regardless of our age.

∞

No one can help you in life unless you have the desire to help yourself first. Your desire allows for spiritual teachers, messengers, gurus, and others to come to you and help you evolve in higher consciousness.

Chapter 2

Life Changes

Our world is getting better and slowly changing through our higher consciousness. We are becoming more helpful with each other. Large and small business corporations are more transparent and helpful towards their employees, and our world is healing itself through climate change. Unfortunately, TV is always showing negative news to scare people even though there is good news happening, but most of the time they are not showing us.

Life changes are a natural, internal, and spiritual process providing great opportunities for you to evolve. In many ways, you are consciously or unconsciously co-creating and being responsible for the life changes you experience. You may experience life changes through a near-death experience, an accident, the passing on of a loved one, career change, or simply feeling internally empty. When these challenges arise, it can be a sign that your old belief routines are not working and are not spiritually helping you to evolve in life.

Life changes take place during periods of internal disharmony, but by expanding or changing your spiritual perspective, you will stimulate internal harmony. For example, believing in abundance at work or in your personal life will allow you not to compete with others. Competition can create undue stress and unhelpful separation from others. Believing in abundance can be manifested in different forms such as experiencing peacefulness among people, taking care of each other, having enough for everyone to live well, and most importantly loving each other.

Sooner or later, all life transitions move you forward through your soul's higher consciousness. The speed at which you can step into higher consciousness is up to you.

I would like to share the following spiritual perspectives to shift your mind-set in order to evolve into higher consciousness:

Life changes can help you alter your old beliefs and routines to overcome your fears and negative behavior. When you defy the fear of change, you realize that change is the process with which you can evolve in consciousness. If you keep believing or telling yourself that change is hard to do, it becomes hard to do. Not evolving spiritually, or feeling stuck, is a habit imprinted deep in your subconscious by your beliefs. It keeps you in your comfort zone without evolving. Once you have the desire to evolve, you will attract the help of others you need in order to change.

∞

When you experience something going wrong in your life, stop, step back, relax, and allow your intuition to guide you through it. A drastic life change may be a wake-up call to change your old ideas that have been passed onto you by your own religious institutions, governments, or family.

∞

When you resist life transitions it is because your subconscious mind (habits) gets in the way of evolving. Embrace changes for a more fulfilling life. Keep updating your mind's old perspectives through spirituality (evolving through higher consciousness) to become more optimistic about life and find solutions for the challenges you are facing. The more you spiritually evolve, the more you experience higher consciousness. Then you will bring internal balance to this world.

∞

It is not important how the outside world is changing or what is happening externally. What is important is how you respond to the change, so it does not affect you. Where there is problem in the world keep yourself peaceful because your peacefulness will contribute to less challenges in your world.

Be aware that you are always shifting or changing at every moment at the thought level, so accept the change and go with the flow of life to evolve. Become more accepting, forgiving, and compassionate with yourself first, then help others in need.

∞

When you ponder life's challenges, you realize they are not challenges at all; they are the result of your mind's old perspectives creating obstacles to spiritual growth. In other words, there are no mistakes in life just more lessons to learn. Questioning your old perspectives is a method of connecting to your higher consciousness. Quieting your busy, inquisitive mind will stimulate your soul's quest for answers through meditation.

∞

Spiritual growth is a slow process that requires you to go with the flow of your own life, so take your time, don't rush, and be patient with yourself. Studying spirituality makes you eventually aware of your intuition to overcome your challenges.

Chapter 3

Our Mind

We have been following our ancestors' belief routines for so long that we accept as truths outdated perspectives. Through conditioning, the lives and experiences of our ancestors are held in our minds and bodies subconsciously, so we have become fearful about life and emotionally and spiritually repressed.

The mind is the storehouse of unlimited thoughts throughout every cell of our body, our subconscious mind (muscle memory), and our soul's consciousness creating our behavior. Making conscious choices, and deciding what is best for us, can help our society evolve in consciousness.

We are a part of the mass consciousness and contribute greatly to what the world creates and experiences through our mindset and behaviors. Through our thoughts, we play a part in the creation of society's well-being. The mind can be our best friend or our worst enemy. We can contribute to the grandest peace or the worst wars. Through our free will we can re-create our spiritual perspectives, and live in peace in our world.

Below, are some perspectives about the mind that can help us understand ourselves better:

Great minds listen to their soul's inspirations to enlighten themselves and help others. You find knowledge in your mind and wisdom in your soul.

Make decisions based on your present moment rather than your past experiences.

∞

By changing our perspective, we can help ourselves and others overcome daily challenges. Through new perspectives of unity, we can evolve faster. If you keep reminding yourself that you are a worthy person that is exactly what you will become.

∞

Our ego is part of our mind, the individuated us; it allows us to experience ourselves and who we desire to be in every present moment. Our ego can help us to spiritually evolve if we train ourselves to be more positive and be one with others.

A false ego, on the other hand, generates separation and a sense of superiority over others, as well as an attitude of usually being right (a sign of insecurity). If we are on an "ego trip," we will keep arguing with everyone. Consequently, if we are ego-invested, it will take us longer to evolve in consciousness because we are not open to changing ourselves or considering other perspectives.

∞

The mind doesn't understand the present moment because it resides in memories of the past. While our minds hold past views, our physical body reflects our current belief routine, and our soul holds future possibilities for better outcomes. Expressing our soul's perspective, such as forgiveness, can heal our past negative experiences.

∞

The mind has been in the comfort zone of our old belief routines for too long. Thus, the mind can hold us back from evolving. When we desire to grow, we will get out of our comfort zone and allow ourselves to make a transition and find our spiritual truth.

∞

Thinking too much makes us less aware of our internal beingness and our external surroundings, and thus distracts us. If we acknowledge the present moment by observing and feeling rather than over-thinking, we will become more aware of ourselves and our surroundings.

∞

An introvert's mind, busy with the internal aspects of life, may find solutions through the creative soul more quickly than an extrovert's mind, which is busy or distracted by the external aspects of life.

∞

Making negative judgments through our minds about others will project that energy onto them, thus not allowing them to change. To help others while they make their transitions, send positive energy such as love rather than projecting ideas of right and wrong onto them.

∞

Our minds can evolve faster with others who are spiritually more evolved, because it can help us remember who we really are: magnificent beings.

∞

Our thoughts project in all directions faster than the speed of light. Positive or negative thoughts will manifest themselves and create outcomes. What you put out you will attract and manifest.

∞

Being overly sentimental binds us emotionally to our past. Sentimentality can hinder our spiritual evolution because it doesn't move us forward. Remember, life is always ahead of us.

∞

The evolution of the mind is mainly spiritual. However, when we spiritualize our minds, we will treat our bodies better—eat more nutritiously, exercise, reduce stress—and become healthier.

∞

Our spiritual perspectives can be a superb tool to create our grandest spiritual experiences when we start evolving through our soul. If we keep reminding ourselves that we are divine beings and love, we will experience this.

Chapter 4

Our Old Belief System

Our old and conventional belief systems have not been working out for people. Outmoded ideas have not produced a spiritually evolved society; instead, we have caused wars and chaos. Old ineffective opinions are so imprinted in our collective consciousness that we are compelled to repeat the same mistakes over and over.

But now, our world's higher consciousness is becoming brighter, and people are becoming more aware and using this energy. We are slowly taking more responsibility for our actions and teaching others to do the same. We are already beginning to use more spiritual perspectives, producing constructive experiences to heal, change, and unite everyone as one family in this world.

I have slowly changed my old belief routines of my parents into more spiritual awareness, and my life now has become easier and more at peace.

I would like to share some old perspectives so you can change them into a new experience:

If you believe you are not good enough, you may experience challenges receiving life's abundance through others. If you believe in the goodness of life or Spirit, you will receive what you need. Believing in the abundance of everything allows you to receive and share what is already here at the physical or spiritual level. Thus, you will no longer fear losing anyone or anything; you will simply accept and wish the best for everyone.

∞

As long as you believe we are separate from each other, you will repress your compassion and not be able to help others in times of need. Help yourself spiritually and physically first and then help others when they need you. Compassion is giving and sharing your mental, emotional, and physical comfort with others.

∞

If you believe that something is hard to do, it will be a challenge because that is what you believe. If you believe something can easily be done, it will be done through your past experiences or creative soul.

∞

Your old belief system about life may contribute to your current challenges. If you keep solving your problems with violence you cannot evolve spiritually but will only create more problems in the world. Violence is a fear demonstrated.

∞

Being bored is another form of anxiety, stress, procrastination, depression, or disconnection from your internal and external worlds. Losing the desire for life can lead to boredom. You may stop taking care of yourself, causing your health to slowly decline, which will make you ill. A spiritual intervention or practice can improve the desire for life. Doing something you love can alleviate boredom, so you can begin to become excited about life. Never give up on what you love.

∞

Why do bad things happen to good people? Bad things can happen to anyone who has not yet learned to listen to her/his gut feelings (intuition) and prevent outside danger. Sometimes bad things also happen for a greater good that we can't yet see or understand. In addition, if we have not overcome challenges from past reincarnations with our loved ones, our loved ones will come into our lives to repair what we have not resolved. We are all co-creating everything with others—the good and the bad. Everyone in our life is a spiritual messenger/angel because they can help us be aware of who we are or who we are not.

∞

A mid-life crisis is another form of feeling spiritually empty. In other words, you are feeling dissatisfied, stressed, or anxious about life. You believe that you may have attained material things and a high degree of education but are still unfulfilled. You feel something is missing and believe your life is stagnating or going downhill. Spirituality, however, can bring awareness into your life and internal harmony by helping you realize what your true spiritual identity is: love.

∞

You cannot erase your past thoughts from your mind and soul no matter how hard you try. At the energy level, your past exists simultaneously within your present and future moments. All your present memories and past experiences are creating your physical reality through your subconscious mind that you have stored. To move forward into the future more peacefully, embrace a spiritual and more inclusive perspective and remain in the present moment. Your present moment, intentions, and actions will create your future.

Chapter 5

The Power of Illusions

Illusions are opinions based on stories or superstitious ideas about life that our ancestors have passed down to us. Due to old ideas of organized religions and governments, many people have been taught to believe that illusory concepts such as hell, evil, condemnation, death, revenge, ignorance, insufficiency, competition (another form of fear), judgment, punishment, jealousy, separateness, and superiority really exist.

These illusions have caused a great deal of mental suffering (lower consciousness), unnatural fear, violence, and separation among people. Accepting these illusions as truth has hurt people mentally, emotionally, physically, and spiritually. As a result, their efforts to evolve spiritually have been frustrated.

Establishing a spiritual education in every school and home will provide access to spiritual wisdom, and enable our society to evolve as one family.

I would like to share some perspectives on illusions so you can challenge them:

Ignorance is an illusion. Your soul, which is pure consciousness/self-awareness and pure energy, knows everything, sees everything and has everything. Ignorance is the state of being consciously and spiritually unaware. Spiritual unawareness may lead to destructive behavior.

∞

Negative judgment, condemnation, and punishment are illusions created around the belief that a mythological or religious God supports these behaviors. This is not the case. God in every myth and religion is love. God doesn't think or behave like a human but demonstrates unconditional love for everyone and everything. If you believe that God is outside of yourself, then you cannot internalize God. God/Spirit lives within you at the energy level.

∞

Insufficiency/lack is an illusion because there is an abundance of everything for everyone in this Earth. Poverty, likewise, is an illusion. When you have enough to eat, a place to sleep, and clothes to wear, you have tapped into the source of abundance and can live well.

∞

Imperfection is an illusion that takes away self-confidence and self-identity and gives rise to doubt. This creates a perfect excuse to repeat mistakes from past experiences and feel inferior. Don't define yourself by what is wrong with you; instead, remind yourself every day that you are a magnificent spiritual being. Remember, in this universe, everyone and everything is perfect because everyone and everything was created out of love by the Spirit.

∞

Worry is an illusion made up by the mind: it is the anticipation of feeling unsafe about something or someone. When you worry, you are consciously making the choice to pay attention to the challenge and not to the solution.

If you keep consciously or unconsciously choosing to worry about someone or something, this will increase this energy and it will become stronger. This worry-energy will materialize and produce behavior in you, such as calling the person you worry about, being concerned about her/his whereabouts and well-being, etc. Your peace has then been repressed by your worries. Step back, relax, and get peace of mind back into your life by wishing this person well or by sending vibes of love. For instance, imagine that you are embracing this person with love through your soul.

∞

Your ideas of superiority create separateness and limit compassion for those in need. Superiority is an illusion. We are all one magnificently divine being. Oneness cannot be superior or inferior to itself, but only spiritually equal.

∞

Need is an illusion. You don't need anyone or anything in order to be happy—just choose to be happy, choose to enjoy love, choose to have anything and everything without needing anything! Needing emotional security from another is an illusion, and needing others to feel good about yourself may lead to low self-esteem. When you love and know yourself spiritually, or believe in yourself, you will have emotional security and won't depend on others.

∞

The idea of loneliness is an illusion made up by the mind. You cannot spiritually separate yourself from anyone or anything; we are all one at the spiritual and physical levels. You are connected to everyone and everything at the energy level. The idea of loneliness doesn't allow you to be happy; it lowers your immune system, reduces your energy, and may affect your health. You are never on your own because your Creator/Spirit, angelic beings, and your multidimensional spiritual guides, (part of your soul from previous and many reincarnations left behind in this physical form, your loved ones who passed on before you from this present and past lives are always with you) helping you in time of need. This is the universal system!

∞

Stress is an illusion, a negative reaction (low vibration) in the mind that has been passed down to you by others. When you are under pressure from others at work or in your personal life, don't take things personally. Relax and be in the present moment. Engage your creative mind to find solutions to your challenges without getting upset. Practice optimism. Creativity is another word for intuition.

∞

Power or control over others is an illusion because it creates dependency. When you give up power over others you are giving up the illusion of control. Only then, can you experience true inner freedom. In the work environment power or control over others doesn't allow them to be creative, but just to follow rules.

∞

The battle between good and evil is an illusion to justify conflict with other countries. The illusion of an enemy has created separation, pain, and wars among nations.

∞

Economic achievement and lifestyle success are illusions produced by a materialistic society. These illusions represent ideas that everyone in the world needs to strive for something more: "I want to be rich," "I want a bigger house" and so on. Wanting material things is usually a sign of covering up spiritual emptiness. Having enough and being content with yourself can help you be less concerned or stressed about material things. Material things should never own you.

∞

Superstitions are cultural illusions produced by unnatural fears that you have co-created with others. Good luck and bad luck don't exist; rather, there are creators and co- creators working in tandem. Your reality is something you are making up in your mind through your mind's perspective. There is no such thing as one reality, only how you perceive your own reality, and how others perceive theirs. Reality is your faith, trust, and belief in action—it is something that feels right.

∞

Get rid of your guilt, and your belief in karma, because they are lower consciousness, indictments, and illusions that don't allow you to evolve. We all do good and bad things sometimes in this physical life of duality (free choice of light or dark) in order to find out who we are. We are all divine beings looking to experience and elevate our higher consciousness.

∞

Expectations of others are illusions that can produce limitations, and limitations reduce your internal spiritual experiences and freedom. When you have expectations, your mind imagines it needs someone or something outside of you to improve a given situation. Expectations reduce your spiritual freedom to be yourself; freedom is living your life without expectations. However, through affirmations you can say out loud the following: "Today I expect a good day," A healthy day," A prosperous day," or "An awareness day." The more you repeat these affirmations, the more they are going to materialize, because repetition creates your truth.

Expectations of others can make you unhappy and frustrated and can eventually harm your mental, emotional, and spiritual state. Expectations come from past experiences based on fears through a limited mindset. Others don't make you unhappy; your expectations do. Accepting others for who they are can help you reduce your expectations of them. This will help you become more tolerant and compassionate with yourself and others. When you lower your expectations, you no longer react negatively to others' behavior. Your ego is no longer invested in what others say, do, or have.

Reducing your expectations in your love life helps you co-create long-lasting relationships. Acceptance is not surrendering or giving up control, but rather accepting your partner for who they are in the moment. This will bring more peace of mind into your life.

∞

Death is an illusion. No one ever passes away. Spiritually, our soul lives forever. When we leave this physical world, we are going to wake up in another spiritual world from a physical dream or a nightmare into a different dimension (heaven). And when we return or reincarnate into this physical world, we are also waking up from a spiritual and joyful dream.

Chapter 6

The Concept of Time

In today's fast-paced society, time is a linear perspective that has been passed down to us by our ancestors. "I have no time," "I need more time," "Time is running out," "Time is money." False beliefs about time keep us rushing around, meeting deadlines, or being unable to think straight. The belief that there is not enough time creates constant stress, and this, in turn, affects our mental, emotional, and physical health.

Below, I would like to share some perspectives about time so you can enjoy life without rushing:

Time is a perception and an illusion; it is a mental construction made up of the limited perception of your mind. Time is here and now in every moment. Use it to reinvent a new you.

∞

When you experience deep meditation, it seems that time goes quickly, and the body rejuvenates. Similarly, when someone or something has kept you so focused that you didn't measure the passage of time, time seems to stop. Time is the eternal present moment going in a circle.

∞

Your past, present, and future moments are happening simultaneously at the energy level. Here and now can help you create a new reality when you acknowledge that time doesn't exist. For example, when you have experienced a memory from your childhood in your present moment, you are reliving that aspect of yourself again at the thought or energy level. If you keep constantly choosing to relive your memories, whether they were good or bad, then it is going to be hard for you to evolve into higher consciousness.

∞

When you take time and go with the flow of this life, everything opens. If you are rushing, you are going against the flow of life, and everything gets in your way. Take your time when you are evolving. What is the rush? The understanding of eternal life allows you to live without rushing or stressing yourself out. Take your time to enjoy life while you are evolving, and being in the present moment, time becomes timeless.

∞

Your physical body ages faster because of your perception of time and your routines. Most people work and retire by the age of sixty-five or seventy. Afterward, you stop taking care of yourself, your health may start going downhill because of a lack of energy, boredom, depression, anxiety, and stress. However, you can live longer when you are joyful, peaceful, loving, and healthy with friends and family. You can improve your life and keep your mind sharp by walking, running, learning how to dance, learning a new language, and continuing to work at what you enjoy.

The more you worry about your age, the more you may grow older, possibly causing you to be afraid of aging or dying. When you stop thinking about your age, you will feel younger, optimistic, have self-confidence, and be healthier. Your age is just a number that doesn't mean much. How you feel is what matters. Keep mentally and physically active, and if you enjoy yourself, you will feel rejuvenated.

∞

Be peaceful in times of confusion and you will find solutions to your challenges.

Chapter 7

Toxic Lies, Doubt, and Trust

From the beginning, lying has been a part of our unevolved culture as a survival mechanism. Lying finds a way into our highest institutions. Lying is in our DNA. However, even if it is in our DNA, we still have the choice to lie or not.

As a kid, I sometimes lied to my mother when she asked if I had done my homework before heading off to play soccer with neighborhood friends. For some reason, my mother always knew when I was lying—probably because lying stimulates physical reactions in the body. I would look away or blush. Later, I paid the price of lying by passing school with only a C average. This didn't bother me at the time; I was not crazy about school. But looking back, although lying may have gotten me what I wanted in the short term, it didn't serve me in the long term.

Below, I would like to share some perceptions on lying that can help you lie less:

Lying can be a conscious or a subconscious habit. A conscious lie is when we know what we are saying to someone is inaccurate, while a subconscious lie is when we say something automatically without thinking about it.

∞

We may bend the truth to manipulate those around us to get what we want—perhaps we believe we need material things, or someone, or something—because lying may help us get that person or thing more easily than telling the truth. Sometimes we fabricate little lies to get money or power. Some people go further—masterminding schemes to deceive and displaying false emotions and information to get what they want. But in the long run lying most always backfires.

∞

We lie to ourselves and others because we don't have the courage to admit the truth. By becoming more spiritual we can learn to express our truth, because out truth is our higher consciousness.

∞

We lie so we will not be negatively judged, condemned, punished, or hurt by others.

∞

We lie to others because we are ego-invested and don't like to be wrong. We lie to get emotional and physical attention from others. When we lie, we may choose to be more aggressive to make others think they are wrong. Lying is a defense mechanism to protect ourselves and others.

∞

We lie to our loved ones in order to get them to stop telling us what to do. If others keep telling us how we should do things, we don't have the free-will to do what we believe is right for us. We also lie to avoid rejection from others.

∞

Lying to a stranger is easier than lying to those we know. White lies are lies nonetheless and will create consequences. All lies are forms of lower consciousness. Sooner or later negative outcomes will occur.

∞

Compulsive lying is an addiction to avoid self-criticism, which causes shame and guilt. A compulsive liar keeps choosing to lie to others because they believe that everyone lies, which gives them an excuse to keep lying.

∞

When we start evolving, we will lie less, because truth brings peace and freedom within ourselves.

Doubt

Uncertainty, anxiety, depression, and insecurity produce the loss of desire for life, doubt and skepticism, which can hold us back from evolving. Losing the desire to evolve will create procrastination and more doubts. When we have a strong desire to evolve spiritually, our energy naturally increases to a higher level; we feel motivated and enthusiastic. Increasing our spiritual perspectives and experiences allows us to transcend doubt and live in faith. Life, in turn, unfolds better for us.

I would like to share some perspectives about doubt, which can help us become more confident about ourselves:

Doubt is another form of fear from unsuccessful past experiences stored in our subconscious mind. Doubt can hold us back from making personal decisions and taking action. If we are mentally and emotionally dependent on others, we will become dysfunctional. By working on our self-identity and self-confidence, we can overcome our doubts to speak the truth.

∞

Doubt manifests itself through old minds' perspectives and negative past experiences of ourselves. If we keep doubting, we project this uncertain energy outward and attract similar experiences, which cause us to doubt even more. We need to know the goodness and worthiness in ourselves.

∞

Getting in touch with our higher consciousness through daily meditation will help us transcend doubt. When we stop listening to our fear (lower consciousness), we will overcome most of our doubts.

∞

Spiritual practice allows us to trust our inner truth, our higher consciousness.

Trust

Trust is mostly a gut-feeling: the knowing that something is true about someone or something. This gut-feeling is our soul, making us aware of an invisible truth about a person or situation. Trusting others can be challenging if we don't know them well. But we possess a powerful tool to help us sense the truth in some situations: our intuition. Our intuition is our sixth sense: knowing or feeling what is true or what is not. Intuition manifests itself in the physical body as a feeling often experienced throughout our upper bodies, and primarily in the stomach area, which is why intuition is often referred to as a gut-feeling.

We may rarely use our intuition because we have been taught to mistrust this sixth sense. Trusting ourselves can be a challenge; it can be easier to trust others to tell us what to do. Practicing tapping into our intuition through daily meditation can help us become wiser and more trusting of ourselves.

I would like to share the following spiritual perspectives on how to improve our self-confidence:

Trusting our feelings and making decisions in every present moment can lead us to a more peaceful and fulfilling life. Our feelings can guide us to a better life tomorrow because they can make us remember that we are making positive choices.

∞

Trust is mindless because it is our intuition taking over during our life's challenges. When our soul is communicating with us through a gut-feeling, we can honor our gut-feeling and take action to find truth (higher consciousness).

∞

Choosing to blindly trust others above ourselves is a sign that we have not yet improved our self-identity and self- confidence. Choosing to trust others first is a sign of self- deception.

∞

Not needing anything from anyone allows us to trust ourselves and help others without expectations.

∞

Training ourselves to trust our soul through daily meditation will encourage us to become aware of our soul's wisdom. Silencing the mind will connect us to our intuition and creativity.

∞

When we remember, acknowledge, and trust the wisdom within ourselves, our fear will lessen. To trust ourselves is to find our inner guidance that will lead us to enlightenment.

Chapter 8

Our Spiritual Emotions

Emotions are energy in motion triggered by thoughts, desires, traumas, joys, memories, etc. to express and survive in this physical form. However, in this physical reality there are just two emotions: love and fear. The rest of the emotions, such as sadness, envy, and anger, are
variations of the love and fear emotions. All emotional experiences are stored in our subconscious mind throughout our body which creates our behavior. All repressed emotions can create stress, rage, and destructive behavior. If we are emotionally attached to our negative past experiences (addicted to old consciousness), we cannot move forward spiritually. Whether we are experiencing love or fear, our emotions are the driving force behind our daily activities.

When we are in touch with our soul's consciousness, we are going to express one emotion: love (higher consciousness) for everyone.

When we start evolving spiritually, we naturally choose love over fear because love is the highest energy in the universe. Loving unconditionally produces energetic upward motion, creating positive outcomes. However, fear causes energy to move downward, which produces negative experiences.

When endeavoring to acquire different skills in life, it is important to remember that self-development is not only intellectual but also emotional. Whether we want to become proficient in healing, social work, dancing, art, or any other pursuit or profession, it is important to understand our natural emotions. Being fearful, insecure, or angry blocks our intuition and the desire to work with people. Expressing, rather than holding back, our natural emotions such as love, envy, fear, anger, and sadness can improve our confidence and intuition, which in turn can make us ready to evolve in consciousness even more.

Emotions are projected outward in all directions throughout the world and the universe. When our soul departs from Earth and returns to Heaven (another dimension, right here, right now), we take our one natural emotion that is unconditional love through our soul so we can express and communicate with other souls and loved ones.

Love

Love is all there is in this universe. It is our true identity. Loving unconditionally and accepting others are expressions of the highest consciousness of Spirit and your Soul. Love is a spiritual reality and an ultimate truth in a purest form of life. The more you express and experience love for yourself and others, the more you raise your energy into higher consciousness. If you repress your love, you can become controlling and possessive (another form of fear). Unnatural fear can close the heart and mind; love opens both.

Love, compassion, and kindness for the self-allow you to take care of yourself and others. Loving yourself increases your desire to live well and be healthy, while not loving yourself can decrease your desire to live. You cannot find love in your mind. You are made of love at the energy level.

Envy

Envy is a natural emotion that can motivate you to be more than what you are and have more than what you have. Expressing your envy for what others have in a positive way encourages you to seek growth and self-improvement. Envy conveyed as admiration, in such language as, "I wish I had your lifestyle," "I wish I could be like you when I grow up," or "Show me how you got there," can be positive and further your spiritual growth. If you suppress your envy, you can become jealous of others.

Anger

Anger is a natural emotion that, if expressed in an effective way, can be constructive. Anger (fear demonstrated) allows you to notice when your boundaries are being disrespected, or to express your expectations, disappointments, or defend your ideas about life. If you repress your anger over the years, it can escalate into rage (destructive emotion) that can lead to negative consequences—especially if others turn your rage back upon you. Anger (fear demonstrated) can make you rigid in your thinking and unwilling to admit your mistakes. Becoming verbally assertive and understanding your spirituality can defuse any negative situation. If you are mindful of not judging yourself and others, you can eliminate most reasons for anger.

Sadness

By embracing and openly expressing your sadness, you can reconcile your feelings after breakups, separations, and good-byes, and even after the death of a loved one.

Suppressing your sadness over the years can cause chronic depression (destructive emotion that lower your immune system) which can affect your health such as your lungs. Sadness can also lead to procrastination making you lose the desire to socialize or to improve yourself.

Suffering from someone's death is a distorted idea or a negative reaction you have created about a loved one who passed. You have created the worst-case scenario in your mind which led you to suffering. Know that the souls of your loved ones are doing well in heaven and part of their souls stay with you. We all go to heaven after we leave this physical life. Embrace their new journey.

Fear

Fear is your friend and a natural emotion. It takes care of you, causing you to step back, be aware, and withdraw from potentially harmful situations. You can feel instinctual fear in your gut; this is your internal radar perceiving danger and sending you warnings. The more you repress your natural fear, the more you accumulate fearful energy around you and the more susceptible you become to developing a chronic sense of despair. Then, when you are feeling mentally or emotionally stressed or under pressure, or when someone or something triggers your fear, you may lose control and act desperately, or experience panic attacks.

Unnatural Fears

Unnatural fears such as fears of losing material things, guilt, abandonment, death, etc. are illusions that have been passed down to us through our parents' and ancestors; old perspective or religious convictions. Anxiety (repressed fear) is another form of unnatural fear. It is negative anticipation of any future outcome. Focusing on the present moment or verbally expressing these fears, can help lessen your anxiety.

Traumas (emotional wounds of the past) can make you disconnect from your inner-self and make it harder to overcome these challenges. A professional spiritual life coach or therapist may be needed to overcome traumas.

Stress (destructive energy) is a form of unnatural fear, can be dangerous to your mental, physical, emotional, and spiritual health. If someone is stressing you out or rushing you, relax. Don't overanalyze. Instead, be alone and focus on the present moment and find a creative way to solve your challenges. Stress is an unnatural fear that can lower your immune system, making you mentally and physically unhealthy over the years.

Making hasty personal decisions in our fast-paced society, often makes our lives more challenging. This is because, on a day-to-day basis, we don't always use the most important tool we brought with us in this life: our soul.

I would like to share a few perspectives on how different decisions can affect your well-being:

Emotions

It is important to be mindful of your emotional state when making a decision. Making decisions when you are angry, for instance, can cause you to be vengeful towards others. By the same token, making decisions when you are sad or depressed can cause you to procrastinate. Making decisions when you are fearful can cause you to make rash choices or act impulsively. Make your decisions when you are calm.

Unconscious

Making unconscious decisions in your personal life based solely on your past experiences or routines may not result in the best outcomes. Instead, make conscious decisions through your feelings in the present moment.

Mind

You make decisions through your mind based on the positive and negative experiences of your past. When you experience challenges in the present moment you engage your mind to make decisions, which can often cause you to keep reliving similar past experiences. Living in the moment and making decisions through your gut feeling will be more beneficial. You make decisions using your left-brain (analytical, conditional, unfeeling, conventional, or inflexible outlook), or you make decisions through your right-brain (creative, feeling, spiritual, free-spirited, unconventional, and a flexible outlook). Making decisions with your false ego, wanting to be right while making others wrong, can create negative consequences. Similarly, if you make decisions while under stress, you can create harmful situations. Make decisions when you are calm and spiritually minded.

Group Consciousness

Drawing on society's old mind's perspective, our global consciousness has created a violent world. You, like others, may be influenced by friends, intimate relationships, governments, religions, or old ideas. Are these working for you? If not, making decisions through your own spiritual perspectives can be very powerful. Think globally and connect with others spiritually because global peace starts by being peaceful with yourself first.

Soul

Making decisions through your soul can lead to more awareness and spiritual growth. True feelings are the language of the soul. When you stop engaging your mind and focus on the soul, you will understand that the soul is constantly communicating with you through feelings. These feelings can manifest themselves as intuition or spiritual truth and can be perceived as physical sensations around the heart or solar plexus. If you want to know what is true for you about someone or something, notice the sensation of feeling good or bad, or comfortable or uncomfortable in one of these areas. This is your soul's way of communicating with you. Similarly, your Spirit or soul doesn't say, "I love you" in words but gives you an experience or loving feeling directly through your whole body.

True feelings are produced by your soul's consciousness. Manifesting itself through your brain, mind, and physical body, your consciousness makes you aware of who you really are: Love.

Chapter 9

Expressing Our Internal Love

We have been talking and singing about love for thousands of years without truly understanding its spiritual meaning: where love comes from, or how it really feels in its purest, most spiritual form. We often don't know how to get in touch with, or how to express, this love because we have been looking for love outside of ourselves instead of from within.

Everyone and everything were created out of love in this universe through the Spirit/Our Creator. Love is giving, receiving, and accepting ourselves and others unconditionally. This multidimensional energy called love is our true identity because we were created out of love from the Spirit, and it is the most fantastic feeling we can harness to bring people and nations together.

When we choose to know ourselves spiritually, we will automatically experience love through others. We can celebrate and demonstrate, through physical affection and sexual intimacy, compassion, kindness, acceptance, forgiveness, wisdom, and unity. Love is our soul expressing the most profound and highest aspect of life.

Knowing myself spiritually was the turning point in my life: to know and love myself first before I love others. When you start knowing yourself spiritually as love, divine, perfection, worthy, and Spirit, then you will allow yourself to experience this amazing state of beingness through your love relationships.

I would like to share some brief perspectives about love so you can experience it even more:

All love relationships are cocreated because there is no coincidence, destiny, luck, accident, or God's plan.

∞

Love is the fountain of life and joy, as well as the fountain of youth.

∞

Love is intuitive, an internal experience of your body, soul, and Spirit. When you express the love inside of you, you feel energized, alive, and passionate about life. Love creates harmony in your mind, body, emotions, and soul. It improves your self-confidence.

∞

Love is in your soul and doesn't ask the mind how to love: your soul just gives the experience of loving unconditionally to the self and others. Love embraces everyone and everything.

There are different kinds of love such as the love with your partner, the love for animals, the love of the mother and her child, the love between friends, and the love for the mother nature, etc.

∞

Being in love with yourself is the soul saying to your conscious mind, "Thank you for expressing my light." When you are in love, you bring out the highest energy of the soul and Spirit.

∞

When you are in love, you make time to see others and celebrate life with them. Love allows you to see love in others. Love doesn't mean that you allow others to walk all over you or abuse you. This is not what love is. Love doesn't cause mental suffering, only your old mind's perspective does. Love is a feeling of ultimate freedom.

∞

By loving yourself unconditionally, you become a source of love to others. You will trigger other people's love from within.

Loving yourself creates pleasant experiences and reminds others to love themselves too. Love allows the universe to evolve in consciousness around you; you are creating and attracting whatever you need to keep yourself moving forward to experience the abundance of the universe through love.

∞

Love is the universal language of the soul that can be demonstrated through actions rather than words. Words cannot replace your true feelings of love because words are sounds representing your thoughts about love, which are usually inaccurate. Love that reveals itself through action is more powerful than promises.

∞

Love is the soul celebrating your true inner self through others. Seeing the internal beauty in others is another expression of love.

∞

When someone turns your love on in a love relationship, you will fall in love with that person. Your soul is sending a love signal into your mind and body. In the meantime, a dispute between your soul and mind occurs. You start daydreaming, get butterflies in your stomach, or become forgetful about things. Now, your heart opens, and you become a loving person.

∞

When you experience the love of your partner, there is no need to ask how much she/he loves you; her/his actions are showing how much she/he loves you. Love always triggers happiness, kindness, passion, affection, tolerance, and compassion.

∞

Love is sharing, caring, and allowing your friends to impose on you in times of need.

∞

Love becomes conditional when you invite fear or uncertainty into your relationships, such as the fear of losing your partner, being jealous, being insecure, or needing another. When you allow your mind to deny love, you deny life. What you deny controls you; your mind becomes the enemy of love. When you stop your mind from denying love, love flows naturally within your life. Love for the self can help you to let go of unnatural fear because love resides in a higher vibration.

∞

Love doesn't get you into trouble; your expectations, opinions, and negative judgments about love co-create trouble for you and others.

∞

Infatuation is the mind being obsessed or needy for someone or something. You cannot find love in your mind. You cannot genuinely love yourself or others until you are free from your old mindset and obsession. Once you are free of these restrictions, you can experience the love within yourself.

∞

If you are afraid to love, it is because you are afraid of losing someone. You cannot lose love because love is something you are. Always share what you already have within yourself: love. If you don't like to be loved by others, it is because you have not yet learned to love yourself. Knowing yourself spiritually is the first step to loving yourself before loving others.

∞

If you love yourself physically, you will love others the same way, superficially. However, by loving yourself internally, you attract others with a similar outlook.

∞

You cannot push love away. Love is all there is in this universe.

∞

The way you love yourself is the way you will experience the love of others because what you put out is coming back to you.

∞

You cannot love yourself if you believe you are unworthy, imperfect, guilty, or that you were born in sin. When you love yourself unconditionally, then you will let go of the indictments you have placed on yourself through your ancestors or religious institutions.

∞

Love is your soul escaping your physical reality through a sexual orgasm. Lovemaking is another way to stimulate and experience Nirvana and the highest expression of love. To raise your consciousness is to express love. Sexual healing is the bridge to Nirvana; it is one of the most wonderful aspects of life.

∞

Loving yourself and others unconditionally allows you to break through all barriers that are holding you back from evolving.

∞

When you meet someone for the first time and you feel an instant connection, this indicates that your soul recognizes this person's soul from a previous incarnation. If the connection is strong, you may fall in love with this person again.

∞

Love can change everyone and everything in our world if we choose it.

Chapter 10

Love Relationships

Many of us have had or are still experiencing dysfunctional love relationships because we haven't known ourselves spiritually. This often causes emotional despair among couples. Dysfunctional relationships are caused by expectations of each other, jealousy, need, fear, trauma, insecurity, or not knowing what love really is.

The more people are consciously aware of their intentions before entering into a love relationship—they feel connected, have good chemistry with their partner, are intellectually, physically, sexually, spiritually, and emotionally independent, and have confidence in each other—the more likely the relationship will succeed.

Love is a spiritual reality (truth) that is found in your soul, so you can remind others to experience all the joy, peace, compassion, wisdom, and freedom.

I would like to share the following brief perspectives about relationships in order to improve your love:

Relationships are a blessing and gift from others to you; they offer you an opportunity to reflect on who you are mentally, emotionally, physically, or spiritually. Intimate relationships are to experience closeness, compassion, peacefulness, connection, and love for each other. All love relationships are co-created because in life there are no accidents, coincidences, destiny, or a superior being in charge of your relationship.

∞

In a love relationship it is not about what you are getting out of it, but what you are sharing with your partner. Every relationship is perfect because through being in a relationship with another, you can evolve and be reminded of who you are—love. Therefore, there are no bad relationships, just opportunities to evolve in consciousness.

∞

If you don't accept your partner for who she/he is, then you will try to change her/him. You cannot change what you cannot accept. Accepting your partner for who she/he is, encouraging her/him to be her/himself, engenders freedom, and self-identity, which enables both of you to evolve.

∞

A flexible personality, transparency, trust, and adaptability are the keys to a lasting relationship.

∞

Age gaps in relationships are irrelevant when adult couples are in love with each other. Unfortunately, people keep choosing to jump to conclusions when one partner is much older than the other. So, relationships with large age gaps become taboo without taking into consideration the motives of the two people involved. Love relationships among adults do not discriminate against anyone or anything. When others see that you and your partner are in love, they will eventually accept your relationship.

In addition, if you and your partner have been together in a love relationship in a previous life and decided to reincarnate in this present life to be together again, you and your partner will come back through different families in different years creating a big gap in age. Therefore, don't condemn others when they are in love, but bless them. However, there are couples with big age gaps having a love relationship for monetary, material, or other forms of interests that eventually they will end up breaking up.

∞

Through your decisions and actions in your love relationship, you will create your own happiness or unhappiness. Men often communicate through action rather than words; women generally communicate more verbally through feelings.

∞

Not having a love relationship doesn't mean you are lonely. Being alone can afford you the opportunity to work on yourself and become more spiritually evolved. Loneliness is an illusion. Spirit, soul, Angelic beings, and spiritual guides are always with you helping you in your life. If you are feeling lonely, reach out and call your friends or family, and get together with them.

∞

Wanting a particular someone and doing whatever it takes to have her/him can lead to a dysfunctional love relationship, because someone who is obsessed can become possessive and controlling. Change your ideas about yourself to change your behavior. Give up the illusion of possessing or controlling someone.

∞

If you are being controlled by your partner, you cannot express love. Consciously or unconsciously choosing to obey your partner's rules and ideas can lead to a dysfunctional relationship because by doing so, you may lose yourself. Not being your genuine spiritual self may repress your self-confidence. Empower yourself and your partner—share your spiritual wisdom with her/him. Make a few rules for each other: trust, unconditional love, and acceptance for who she/he is.

When your love relationship has become dysfunctional for so long no matter how much counseling you had in the past, then it is time to move on. Otherwise, both of you are going to be miserable and more dysfunctional.

∞

When you love your partner more than you love yourself, it can be difficult to let go of your relationship if she/he wants to move on with her/his life. Learning to love yourself allows you to be more accepting and to let go of your partner more peacefully. Love is giving your partner unconditional freedom rather than trying to own them.

Letting go of a love relationship can be challenging if you love your partner more than you love yourself. This can happen if you have invested much time and effort in your partner that you have created dependency, and now your partner wants to move on in life because she/he wasn't able to find her/himself with you. If you truly love yourself and your partner, you will let go of your partner so she/he can grow and evolve.

As long as you still hang on to her/him during a dysfunctional love relationship, it will be hard to let go of your partner. You have mentally, emotionally, and physically become attached to your partner, and this has held your partner hostage, so she/he won't let go of you. However, when you let go of your partner, then both of you are freeing yourself from a dysfunctional love relationship into a new and healthier adventure.

∞

Relationships based on physical looks alone without a spiritual component often don't last. You may eventually reject that partner for someone with whom you can naturally evolve in consciousness.

All challenges in your relationships are co-created (the law of attraction) with your partner through illusions of need, expectation, jealousy, etc. There are no broken hearts in relationships, just expectations you or your partner may have of each other being unfulfilled. Participating in on-again/off-again relationships is a sign that you are attached to the drama of life. Drama not only keeps you from evolving but also encourages you to repeat the same mistakes again and again.

∞

When you enter a new love relationship it can be difficult at the beginning because you may be bringing emotional baggage or traumas from unfinished past love relationships. But, if one of you is matured or spiritually more evolved, then you can make your love relationship work, and help your partner evolve. This way you can have a good and lasting love relationship.

∞

When you enter a new love relationship, you and your partner may bring in several personalities. Trauma from past toxic relationships, insecurities, vestiges from childhood traumas, and anxieties can bombard your relationship. Love and compassion can conquer all these challenges and bring unity for both of you to heal.

∞

Rage, jealousy, and possessiveness imprison your loved ones. Reject jealousy and possessiveness, they are illusions. Jealousy derives from fear and insecurity and is demonstrated when one partner feels insecure about the actions of the other. But you can overcome your jealousy by becoming unconditionally loving and allowing her/him to be who they are. If the situation doesn't resolve, you may need to move on.

∞

When you allow your partner to be emotionally, mentally, or physically abusive toward you, it is usually because past trauma has caused you to become desensitized to emotional or physical pain. Perhaps you don't believe you deserve better. This can stem from not yet loving yourself spiritually; in other words, you are attracting what you need to heal and evolve. Spirituality helps you evolve into higher consciousness, gain self-love, self-confidence, and self-identity to heal your trauma wounds and break the cycle of abusive relationships.

Many intimate relationships become dysfunctional because your old belief system is no longer working for you. However, by changing your belief system or perspective about life into a more spiritual one, you can restore your intimate relationship into a more harmonious one. For instance, overcoming your insecurity, jealousy, possessiveness, or your need to be in control, can allow you to express unconditional love.

∞

If you want to improve your relationship, it is important to not have unreasonable expectations of her/him, which will create unhappiness and resentment. Being compassionate, unconditionally loving, and nonjudgmental will help you resolve your conflicts.

∞

Not loving yourself can make it challenging for you to love another. Moreover, not loving yourself may lead to needing more attention from others. Complaining, judging, getting angry, victimizing yourself through others can also lower your energy. Having compassion for yourself can be an opportunity to start loving yourself and improving your self-confidence.

Compassion creates unity.

∞

People who lack a strong sense of spiritual self may be sensitive to negative criticism from others, which can lower their energy. When they feel threatened or hurt, they can become angry, violent, or verbally aggressive. They may have lower self-esteem, or not know how to love themselves. Working on their spirituality is the first step to improving their self-esteem.

∞

If you attract individuals who are confident, creative, healthy, joyful, and self-aware but feel you lack these traits yourself, it is possible that you are being reminded to bring out these qualities within yourself. Through these individuals, you can create an opportunity to become more confident, creative, and joyful.

Soul mates of the same or different genders are those who think alike so much that it feels like one or both of them are falling in love with themselves and with each other.

∞

It is not important how long your relationship lasts; it is important that you be genuine to yourself and to your soul (consciousness, motivation, energy) so you can evolve.

∞

Most love relationships are co-created by past actions and current intentions. If you get into a relationship because of need, money, or loneliness, it may eventually unravel. Being honest with yourself in a love relationship can be the key to a joyful experience. Be clear about your intentions as to why you want to be with her/him. Being with someone because you just want to have children, escape family challenges, or be taken care of, is not the way to a serious relationship. In the long run, this kind of love relationship may not work.

Chapter 11

The Miracle of Sex

When we talk about sex and focus only on its physical expression, we don't understand its spiritual meaning.

Sexual tensions may include issues with your own physical body or with your partner's. Your old ideas about sexuality may prevent you from realizing that a loving, sexual relationship can be the most powerful and wonderful way to heal yourself from uncertainties and enjoy life.

Women have been sexualized and traumatized by men throughout history. Even today through movies and music videos etc., so young men have learned to copy such behavior towards women. These old ideas about sex are reinforced by age-old negative perspectives about sexuality, which causes sexual confusion, shame, dysfunction, repression, violence, and rape.

Most women have been sexually, emotionally, and physically repressed by religious institutions for a very long time. But now women are getting to know themselves more internally, are exploring their bodies and claiming their physical, mental, and spiritual integrity. This will enable them to experience more sexual freedom.

Today, many women will not tolerate mistreatment by men in any way. Women are more confident and independent concerning sex and love affairs. Both young men and women are breaking religious, ancestral, cultural, and family rules concerning sex because they know intuitively that it is a wonderful, natural, fulfilling manner of expressing love.

Sex is love in this physical and spiritual manifestation. It is our closest connection to our soul and Spirit/Creator. Demonstrating love through lovemaking produces a deeply meaningful, internal, and personal experience. When you are in love with yourself you will naturally turn on the love of others to remind them who they are. Here are some perspectives about sex that can help you bring unity with your partner:

When you fall in love, sex becomes an outlet for your passion to celebrate life.

∞

Sex is the spiritual love you bring into this physical form through your soul; it is communion and healing between lovers.

∞

Sex/love brings unity and Oneness in mind, body, and soul; it is the highest expression of life. When you achieve higher consciousness through your soul, you experience true love and sex.

∞

When you truly love yourself spiritually, you can experience a higher consciousness of love through an orgasm. It happens automatically when the soul expands itself through love and embraces and heals your physical body at the cellular level.

∞

When you and your partner click mentally, physically, emotionally, and spiritually during lovemaking, your energy centers open, so you can experience union, freedom, Oneness, joy, and love with each other through a sexual orgasm.

∞

A "sexy" person is one who is consciously, physically, and mentally in touch with her/his own sexuality, whether she/he is straight, gay, or lesbian. A sexy person is someone who likes to express her/his sensual body movements in the way they walk, dance, or wear their clothes.

∞

Having sex is a form of self-love. Masturbation, too, is a form of self-love. Self-gratification allows you to release anxiety, experience euphoria, and feel great about yourself. You cannot enjoy sex if you feel guilty, shameful, or fearful. Enjoy sex with passion, eagerness, and freedom—without fear.

∞

When your lover triggers your inner love during intimacy, it will cause you to love yourself and her/him more. Lovers should love themselves before sharing true love with their partners. If a person believes love comes from outside of herself/himself, the focus may be on one's partner and not on oneself. This is not the way to spiritual fulfillment.

When you fall in love with someone, keep the love for yourself alive. Don't let anyone turn it off for any reason. This will be your chance to experience the grandest aspect of yourself. It can also be a great opportunity to make your relationship more joyful.

∞

The experience of mental or physical abuse during your relationship may lead you to lose the desire for sex/love. Spiritual practice to improve your self-confidence and self-identity can help you resolve your conflicts with your partner. As you heal and learn to love yourself spiritually, you will not allow the pattern of abuse to continue in any way. Compassion and kindness for self is the first step to overcoming challenges.

∞

Having different sexual partners may be an indication that you have an addiction, are sexually unsatisfied, or are being deeply ego invested. If you change your perspective about sex through spirituality, your addiction can transcend to preference rather than need.

Loveless sex, or sex without an emotional connection, with different partners outside your principal relationship, is something your false ego needs. You might wish to be unfaithful to your partner because of loneliness, boredom, or insecurity.

Sex addiction without love can be a distorted idea about sex/love or the result of past traumatic experiences that need healing. You may become emotionally or physically attached to this need for recognition, which can prolong the cycle of addiction. Focusing on one partner with whom you feel the most connection can help you let go of the need for promiscuity.

Chapter 12

Friendship

A friend is someone you can trust, respect, impose upon, accept, and love unconditionally. A friendship is a commitment between people to share wisdom, peace, love, and joy, and to help each other in times of need. Maintaining deep friendships is one of the most important features of a strong society.

Having a solid friendship with yourself improves and reflects your friendships with others. It helps you establish a commitment with yourself and others. Creating great friendships helps us create a strong community, which allows us to build effective relationships and partnerships with peoples and nations.

My best and long-term closest friends and I got to know each other very well over the years, and we have been very supportive of each other in times of need. My friends have encouraged me to express my purpose in life, which is love and compassion, and to know myself spiritually. I am always grateful for having them in my life.

I would like to share the following perspectives about friendship so you can become the source of friendship:

Friendship is something you nurture over a long time; nurturing a friend like a family member will allow you both to harvest and enjoy each other's love.

∞

Friends work to encourage and support each other's growth and aspirations. A friend is someone who supports you unconditionally, even if you have opposing points of view. Acquaintances, on the other hand, come and go in your life.

∞

Friends are those who freely impose upon you in times of need; allowing your friends to impose on you is another way of saying you love them. Asking for help or using your friends in time of need can be the fastest way to find out who your friends really are. Best friends can be your best supporters when you go through challenges in life.

∞

When you spiritually evolve, you attract wiser friends. If you attract those who are negative while you are evolving, help them, but don't exclude them.

∞

If you know, trust, love, and help your friends, they will become a part of your spiritual family. If you start a dialog with your friends about spirituality, your friendship will become a powerful bond. Each of you will grow faster and you will help each other and others to evolve in consciousness.

Chapter 13

Similarities Attract

The law of attraction means that whatever you keep projecting or sending out through your energetic thoughts and intentions into this world will materialize.

Through the law of attraction, you become aware that you are your own creator and co-creator with others. As such, you will attract those with similar thought patterns to evolve in consciousness and reshape your life.

The following are some perspectives that demonstrate that similarities attract so you can be more conscious of what you are cocreating with others:

"Like attracts like": People will attract others with similar outlooks as themselves—emotional, intellectual, physical, or spiritual—to improve themselves. The strongest aspect of yourself that you project, you will attract and manifest.

∞

Opposites in personalities attract as well. When you attract someone who has different perspectives from yours it means you may have repressed what the other has developed, such as self-confidence, self-identity, or maturity. This is an indication that you desire to improve yourself through her/him. Opposites in personality can complement each other in the long run.

∞

If you are a self-confident person and attract someone who has lower self-esteem, then it is an opportunity to empower her/him. Likewise, if you attract people who are spiritually evolved, it's an indication that you are ready to evolve, too.

∞

When you condemn yourself and others, you encourage and attract similar behaviors. Don't condemn. Through what we think, say, and do collectively, we create positive or negative outcomes.

∞

Whatever is going to happen in your physical experience is already happening at the energetic level. If you keep choosing, thinking, or being optimistic, this will eventually materialize into your physical reality. This is the law of attraction.

∞

Whatever you fear the most, you will attract and experience, because what you send out and believe, you manifest in a physical form. So, be careful of what you fear.

∞

When you are evolving spiritually, you attract healthy and diverse friends and relationships that keep moving you forward. Likewise, when you are already spiritually evolved, you attract those who want to grow in that way, and you can help them move forward.

Chapter 14

The Human Family

Now that we are making improvements through higher consciousness, we can bring the family together. Family is the greatest cornerstone of unity in the world. Families protect, love, educate, and support each other in times of need. Creating strong family ties brings family members together as a unit and creates a community and a strong society.

Parenting is our natural commitment to our children. If parents continue to spiritually grow, they can help their children and grandchildren evolve so that the next generation can experience fewer struggles, more happiness and peace.

Children are the future of our world; we can improve ourselves as parents by listening to the wisdom children innately bring into life. If we spiritually educate children, they can express their joy, peace, love, compassion, creativity, and inner freedom. They are our hope to heal and change the next generation into a more evolved society.

It is imperative that today's children be exposed to spirituality; all children naturally experience spiritual phenomena throughout their childhood and teenage years. If spiritual instruction were a common part of our educational system, our children would have continual reminders that they are spiritual beings having a physical experience.

I would like to share the following perspectives on how to raise children to become healthier and wiser adults:

Through the energetic vibration of their personalities, the souls of children and parents attract each other at the energy level before they reincarnate into this physical form. Children choose to have personalities similar to those of their parents. They also choose the place, time, the gender, race, culture, and birth order into which they reincarnate in this physical world.

∞

Parents, make joyful conversations with your young children about spirituality and don't be surprised if they may already know the answer to something you don't know. This way you will create a more intimate relationship with them, and you will become closer to each other.

∞

Parents, don't teach your children to follow in your footsteps, but teach them to follow their own passion or whatever gift or talent they bring into this life. This way they can grow and choose what they know intuitively or remember about their past lives.

∞

The first seven years of a baby's life are very important because they learn so much through their parents' body language and behavior that in later adulthood will express similar behavior.

∞

Children want to enjoy life and they know how to enjoy the present moment. Allowing them the freedom to enjoy the present moment will help them to enjoy life as adults.

∞

Commitment to your children should be your priority, regardless of whether your relationships or marriages work. If a relationship with a partner or spouse becomes dysfunctional, you should continue to raise children in a loving environment where they are emotionally protected. This will be healthier for them, whether or not their parents remain together. It is best to maintain friendly terms with an ex-partner for the sake of the children. Grandparents and close relatives can also help raise children to create a strong, extended family for them. As the adage says: "It takes a village to raise a child."

∞

Allow your children to freely express themselves mentally, physically, emotionally, and spiritually so you can get to know them better. Let them cry when they feel sad, even if they are boys. If you tell them to stop crying, you will be forcing them to repress their emotions, and they may have challenges expressing themselves as adults. The more children express their emotions, the healthier they will be.

∞

Criticizing your children and telling them they are not good enough lowers their self-esteem and creates a lack of self-love. Teach your children not to compare themselves with other children. Empower them with kindness, encourage them to do what they love, and support them unconditionally.

∞

Don't punish your children physically or emotionally; this causes trauma, and they may become violent with others as adults. Train them to be peaceful from early childhood.

∞

Don't make your children feel guilty about things they have done; guilt makes them feel small and diminishes their self-identity and self-confidence. Instead, explain to them that there are consequences for the decisions and actions they create with others.

∞

Using money to manipulate your children—to reward them or buy their love—leads to a potentially unhealthy relationship. It is also important not to constantly give in to their demands, because eventually, they may try to control you. Help them, instead, to become self-sufficient and independent.

∞

The more mental and emotional comfort you give your children, the healthier adults they become. When a parent leaves a child to cry alone until she/he falls asleep, the child may develop feelings of abandonment and later as an adult may have challenges letting go of love relationships.

∞

When your children become teenagers, help them understand healthy sexuality. Tell them that protected sex/love is to celebrate life with a partner. This will prepare them to explore love and protected sex for self-gratification in a mature, safe, and nurturing way.

∞

Don't teach your children to fight so they can defend themselves from others. Fighting with others contributes to more violence in the world. Teach them not to react to negative criticism of others. Remind your children that they are love.

∞

As parents, deciding what is best for our children indicates that we are loving ourselves through them. As a result, they may become unhappy and unhealthy. Children need to think for themselves, even if it takes them longer to find out what they want to do with their lives.

∞

Get to know your children's natural talents and help educate them in those areas to become successful adults.

∞

Don't verbally or physically fight with your spouse or your partner in front of your children because they can copy this behavior or develop traumas and affect them in their adulthood.

∞

Don't buy them toys of war: guns, swords, tanks, knives, or violent video games—because this can encourage violent behavior. Having guns in the house while raising children is dangerous. Children don't know the difference between real guns and toy guns. If you have guns in the house, get rid of them for the safety of your family.

∞

Don't take your children to scary movies because this may cause them to become subconsciously afraid of people and situations. Also, don't encourage your children to scare or bully others while playing; this causes mental and emotional trauma, which can be stored in the subconscious mind.

∞

Don't feed your children unhealthy processed food. Keep them healthy by cooking and teaching them to prepare nutritious, healthy meals at home.

∞

Through joy, your children can learn much faster, whether in school or at home; joyfulness makes your children more open-minded to learning. Help your children to find joy in their personal lives and in their work.

∞

Teach your children social skills to develop self-confidence with their friends, so they can have a healthy social life.

∞

Give your children limited access to social media because spending too much time on the internet can be dangerous. Teach them not to talk to strangers online. Children or teenagers may be looking for attention, acceptance, and recognition through social media that they may not be getting from their parents. If your young children are not getting enough love or attention from you, they may start looking for what they need elsewhere. On the other hand, when you are overly protective of your children, they may struggle to grow and can become mentally and emotionally dependent on you and on others. Help children think for themselves by providing them with opportunities to become self-sufficient. Give them tasks they like to do at home. Share your wisdom and help them be responsible for themselves and others.

∞

Remind your children that they are loved, and most importantly, that there is just one family on earth—the magnificent human family. This knowledge will help them connect with others and form meaningful relationships.

∞

Teaching your children to meditate for fifteen or twenty minutes once or twice a day can be beneficial for them. It can lower children's anxiety or stress at home or at school. Meditation is an important tool to help children get in touch with their soul's wisdom and increase their understanding of life.

Chapter 15

Our Divine and Eternal Soul

What is the soul? We have been asking ourselves this question since time immemorial. Most of us still don't have the answer or understand the function of the soul because we have not been taught through our educational system.

The soul/consciousness/intelligence is the essence of life and part of the Spirit at the energetic level, which represents the love that has no beginning and no end. We always have existed along with the Spirit. We are all here in this physical world discovering who we really are through the soul: love.

Most of us have consciously or unconsciously experienced our soul through such phenomena as an out- of-body experience (astral projection) or Déjà-vu. Déjà- vu is an out-of-body experience you may have had in a dream. Your soul has traveled during your sleep to a particular place to bring you awareness and experience, such as "I know I have been here before."

If you believe in reincarnation, you will know that when you come into this physical life, you bring your soul, and all your past incarnations to the energy level. You may be repeating a life like your previous ones, whether positive or negative. If you have evolved in your past lives, you will continue to evolve in consciousness in this present life and so on. In addition, when you come back or reincarnate in this physical form, you will bring your family's group consciousness within your soul in order to feel comfortable with each other. In other words, your grandchildren could have been your parents in your previous life. This is the reason that you feel very close to them and want to take care of them the same way they took care of you in another life.

Below, I would like to share some brief perspectives about the soul so you may be able to experience it:

We are all soulmates reincarnating in this physical form to recreate a spiritual journey together. We are all One Soul without beginning and without end, bound to each forever.

∞

Our soul/consciousness is an expression and self-image of our Spirit/Creator/Love at the energy level. It is our highest state of consciousness and our personal identity: love.

∞

Your soul is the highest state of existence, which allows you to produce immediate experiences from which to choose. When you choose to be happy the soul gives you the experience, and this experience raises your energy.

∞

By enlightening your mind through the wisdom or perspective of your soul/consciousness such as understanding that we are all one family on this earth, we can begin to treat each other with more compassion and in a more loving way.

∞

Your soul yearns to experience the grandest aspects of yourself through your physical reality. Your soul knows everything, sees everything, and has everything.

∞

Your soul can sense and perceive when someone or something is coming through you. When you experience a premonition, your soul's consciousness has already seen it at the energy level, so later, you will experience it.

∞

Your soul/consciousness is wisdom (knowledge experienced) past, present, and future simultaneously. The more wisdom you practice and share with others such as "We are all one", the more wisdom you will remember and attract.

∞

The aura/electromagnetic field of your soul projects your mental, emotional, physical, and spiritual vibration. If you are sensitive or intuitive, you can perceive people's thoughts and emotions. Your soul is always drawing evolved souls into your life, so you can evolve through them.

∞

Your soul will live forever because you are Spirit/Creator manifested. You need not fear death once you realize that the soul never dies.

∞

All souls are spiritual messengers in this universe helping you remember who you are spiritually. If you have not been kind to others, someone will demonstrate her/his kindness to you, to help you remember and trigger your own kindness from within.

∞

The soul usually keeps reincarnating in this physical form through the same families to continue to evolve and help others do the same. The more you evolve in consciousness, the quicker you can choose to reincarnate in this physical form and remember who we were in the past so you can help others evolved.

∞

An "old soul" is someone who has reincarnated many times throughout this physical world and has thus evolved spiritually and will teach others to evolve.

∞

Your joy is your inner child at the soul/consciousness level expressing total freedom at any given moment. Express this joy throughout your life. Look for joyful people who can make you smile or laugh. Laughing or being joyful helps you to stay healthy and optimistic. Joy keeps you internally balanced from a stressful society.

∞

You can become more in touch with your soul through daily meditation. The soul cannot be reached through your rational mind. The mind lives in the past.

∞

The third eye is the window of your soul. It is believed to be housed within the pineal gland, located at the center of the brain. It is your third eye that can see, perceive, and know the truth (higher consciousness) about your soul.

Chapter 16

The Power of Meditation

Meditation is a deep journey into the unknown, where your physical reality meets your spiritual reality. This is your grandest tool and your great opportunity to meet the real you: your soul/consciousness. Your spiritual reality can bring remarkable transitions into your physical reality when you have the desire to evolve in consciousness.

Meditation is a journey into your soul. It is one of the most important tools for spiritual evolution because it is the bridge to connect with your higher consciousness.

There is not a right or wrong way or certain time or place to meditate. It is whatever works for you. You can meditate while you are walking, working, lying down, sitting down, writing a book, painting, dancing, making love, exercising, etc. Meditation is a deep awareness you are experiencing in the present moment through your soul/consciousness.

Meditation is your direct communication to find your wisdom through your soul and Spirit. Practicing meditation allows you to become aware of your soul's purpose, which is love and compassion and to evolve spiritually.

∞

When you are internally at peace with yourself during your daily meditation, you can experience self-healing. This peacefulness allows you to slow down time and rejuvenate yourself at the cellular level.

∞

Daily meditation is the key to experiencing an out-of-body experience. For a more effective meditation, you can visualize all your front and back energy centers moving in clockwise circles to open them up. Then, begin to take several deep breaths in through the nostrils and out through the mouth before meditation. Throughout the meditation—with eyes closed—focus on your breathing and your heart without expecting anything. With practice, you will learn to receive messages in different forms from your soul and Spirit.

∞

Meditation is another form of feeling your love and joy.

∞

A deep meditation is when you stop hearing your breathing, heartbeat, or outside noises: where time seems to stop. People who have out-of-body experiences while meditating cannot hear their breathing or heartbeat because they are stepping out of their physical reality and into a higher and different dimension.

∞

Meditation is an opportunity to be grateful for the abundance of all the good things coming to you.

∞

Meditation is the state of being at one with your soul; it empowers you to spiritualize and revolutionize your old ideas. By practicing meditation, you will feel differently when making personal decisions. This will be a sign that you are changing and maturing, becoming your true spiritual self.

∞

Daily meditation of twenty minutes reduces worries, stress, depression, anxiety, anger, and lowers your blood pressure.

Chapter 17

Beingness for Empowerment

Being joyfully alive is the highest state of existence of your soul. It is your soul's nature to be joyful, and through joy you can evolve faster. If you choose to be happy, you generate a healthy spiritual life and create positive experiences. Remember, you are a human being and not a human minding. However, living your life in your mind (thinking a lot) will allow you to do things thinking that you are going to make yourself happy, but this can create more disappointments.

In beingness, the soul desires to experience the grandest aspect of life—love. Beingness allows you to experience the present moment, here and now, without worrying about yesterday or tomorrow. When you are spiritually true to yourself, aware of yourself, and being yourself, you will evolve faster through joy. You are what you are being, not what you are thinking or doing.

I would like to share the following perspectives about beingness so you can begin to experience it:

Being grateful

Being grateful for the abundance of everything in this world is the highest form of spiritual acknowledgment.

I give thanks for the well-being of my family, for the ability to write this book, to my friends sharing their spiritual and material abundance with me, and to my acquaintances reminding me that they are part of my family. I give thanks for my Spirit allowing me to follow in her footsteps—one step at a time.

Gratitude is the awareness of Oneness with everyone and everything. Giving thanks to others is giving thanks to yourself because you and others are one. I give thanks for the spiritual and material comforts I have.

∞

Gratitude is the awareness that you are already enjoying abundance in life. Abundance is the feeling of the soul and Spirit that you can create enough of everything spiritually and physically for everyone. Being grateful, before and after you have received something or someone, is acknowledging abundance (taking care of each other).

∞

Be grateful for the smallest gesture of kindness. When you are kind to yourself and others, you are truly being grateful. Being polite and courteous is a demonstration of gratitude.

∞

When you believe in abundance and it becomes your truth, you are putting the law of the universe into motion: What you send out at the energy level, whether positive or negative, you will receive in a physical form.

Being optimistic

Being optimistic helps you find answers to your questions and do your best for yourself and others. Your optimistic attitude brings out your creativity to move you forward. Optimism is the joyfulness of your soul running at high speed, delivering answers to your conscious mind. Through the passion, eagerness, and action generated by optimism, your spiritual goals can come true. Optimism is your soul smiling and saying, "I can do it!" and finding solutions to your challenges. When attempting to overcome challenges, place yourself in a state of optimism. Release the belief in failure—it is an illusion. No one can fail in life, but one can have more experiences and not repeat again the same mistakes.

∞

Optimism is faith in action. Optimism generates action and promotes a healthier mental, physical, and spiritual outlook. If you abandon optimism, you abandon faith. Don't lose faith in life because faith is always on your side. Optimism opens your heart and mind to finding conventional and unconventional ways to resolve challenges.

∞

Optimism about life makes you see the bright light in yourself and in everyone else.

Being Happy

It is the nature of your soul to be happy. Choose to be joyous as often as you can, and you will attract more happiness and health. Happiness is who you are within your soul. Happiness is your soul demonstrated. When you are happy, your brain becomes more alert to your soul's inspirations. An open mind makes you aware of your soul's wisdom.

Being happy produces an immediate manifestation of the soul's desire. Merely thinking of doing something happy, on the other hand, slows down the manifestation process because the mind overanalyzes things of the past.

Many people look externally for happiness, expecting others to make them happy. You too may have thought that happiness comes from an outside source. You may have also defined happiness as an accumulation of material things. But do things really make you happy? Have you forgotten that you carry happiness in your soul?

∞

Joy is the fountain of youth. When you experience joy and love, you feel energized, younger, and healthier. Daily joy keeps you healthy and living longer. It connects you to your soul and rejuvenates your heart, mind, and body.

∞

When you believe in your own happiness, it becomes your truth, which creates experiences. Happiness turns your energy into motion, thereby producing more happiness. When you stop reacting to what others are thinking, saying, and doing, you empower your happiness and peacefulness.

∞

Happiness is your soul triggering your brain's endorphins (pain relief), allowing you to feel spiritually and physically positive. When you are happy you create a healthy brain, because happiness is a higher consciousness that positively affects your physical body at the cellular level. When you experience happiness in the present moment, you allow yourself to enjoy life with others.

∞

Nobody can control another person's happiness, but someone who is happy can trigger happiness in others. Triggering happiness in others encourages you to trigger your own joy. Be the happy person in the crowd who inspires happiness. When you express your happiness, your sense of humor becomes unlimited.

∞

Being happy is accepting all things with love. Happiness makes you flexible. Happiness is mindless: it is not something to analyze; it is experienced internally.

∞

Be happy because you are here to celebrate life. Choose in every moment of your highest excitement to accomplish what you enjoy the most. When you start living your excitement in the present moment, it will allow you to attract what you need, because it is exactly what you will project through your thoughts and desires. However, living in the past through your dramas, may not allow you to experience happiness.

∞

Expectations from others can lead to unhappiness and can temporarily affect your mental, emotional, spiritual, and physical state. When you expect actions from others and don't receive them, you are disappointed, especially if you have done something for them and expect reciprocation.

∞

Happiness is a personal choice that impacts your personal and work environments. It allows you to become creative. If you feel unhappy, you lack the motivation to work and you can't serve others well. Unhappiness impedes spiritual growth.

∞

Do things because you are happy, for happiness creates all your circumstances and experiences.

Chapter 18

Spiritual Inspirations

Spiritual inspiration is the wisdom of the soul, the earth, the galaxy, or the universe, and it is energy all around us, waiting for you to tap into. Inspiration allows you to recreate a new spiritual you to evolve.

When I was growing up in Lima, Peru, I was aware of my own spiritual world. I possessed insight into deeper spiritual concepts such as eternal life, souls, and reincarnation. I had not read about these things, and no one had taught me; I just knew. Later in life, I realized that something inside of me was showing me these spiritual perspectives, and I began to understand that this spiritual inspiration came from my soul.

My knowledge of the spiritual realm inspires me to remember who I was, who I am, and who I will become on my evolutionary path. As a spiritual life coach, Reiki master, and a ballroom dance instructor, I share my spiritual inspirations and experiences with others so they may improve their lives.

The following are some perspectives on inspirations:

You are a divine being born perfect. We are one family on this earth. What you put out; you will attract. There is abundance in this universe. Your soul is always happy, peaceful, loving and free.

Inspirations are another form of your soul reminding you of who and what you are: an eternal spiritual being in this physical and spiritual world. Spiritual inspirations are the universal language of life.

∞

When your mind and heart desire inspiration, your soul responds by giving you wisdom.

∞

Inspirations are always constructive, coming from your soul and all around to guide you in your life. They can produce positive experiences.

∞

Inspiration comes when you are in love with life and with yourself, when you are being creative (creativity is another word for intuition), or doing things you love. Spiritual inspiration can come anytime, anywhere, through a peaceful state of mind or meditation.

Here are some spiritual perspectives to help you become more aware of yourself:

Spiritual awareness is the mind becoming enlightened about who and what you are. When you become aware, you can produce different, more spiritually advanced experiences in your life. Enlightenment is another word for awareness or remembering.

Spiritual awareness is a form of intuition/knowingness of a truth about someone or something. Spiritual awareness can awaken your mind to overcome personal challenges.

∞

Being spiritually aware in every moment produces immediate, joyful experiences, because your intentions and actions can move you anywhere you wish to go in life. Be all that you can be at the spiritual level. Living in the present moment allows you to experience who you desire to be Love.

∞

When you are aware of who you are spiritually, you remind others of what you are becoming: a spiritual being. This allows others to follow in your footsteps and become more spiritual as well.

∞

Through your own spiritual awareness, desires, and decisions, you have the power to change your future experiences. Your internal spiritual power is ready to be released. Act now and create the spiritual future you desire! Your daily choices and actions produce your future experiences.

∞

Everyone and everything brings you awareness of your spiritual self. Some people make you aware of who you were in your past life. Some people make you aware of who you are in the present. And some people make you aware of your possible future.

∞

Don't condemn those who are spiritually unaware. Instead, support them in their spiritual growth and help them become aware of their true identity—they are still living in the illusions of their ancestors. Help them to wake up.

∞

It is just as important to be creative as it is to be intelligent. Creativity encourages you to solve challenges. Intelligence (information) helps you to know what your options are. When you choose creativity, it is your soul that helps you to make wiser decisions.

∞

Self-discovery can lead you into mastering your own spiritual life so you can choose and experience love.

Chapter 19

Our Amazing Spiritual Energy Centers

Originating from Sanskrit, the word chakra means wheel or circle. These are the spiritual energy centers our soul brings into this world when we are born to help us mentally, emotionally, and spiritually balance our physical body. To maintain optimum health, it is essential to incorporate the spiritual, mental, and physical components of the energy centers into the self-healing process. Remember, we are all energy/soul.

When I was twenty-three years old, a spiritual healer introduced me to the concept of the human body's energy centers or chakras. As I trained in the art of Reiki energy healing, I came to believe that our energy centers are spiritual manifestations of our soul's consciousness.

The seven most well-known energy centers are lined up about three to four inches apart from each other. The first energy center is located at the base of your spine and the seventh energy center is on top of your head. This first energy center moves vertically downward toward the ground in a circular motion, and the seventh energy center moves upward in a circular motion. The second, third, fourth, fifth, and sixth energy centers move outward horizontally in a circular motion.

When the energy centers are moving in different directions from each other, it indicates that a person is mentally, emotionally, or spiritually confused. When some of the energy centers move diagonally towards the right-brain, it may imply a feminine inclination. Conversely, when some of the energy centers move diagonally towards the left-brain, it may indicate a masculine inclination, whether you are female or male.

You can open a person's energy centers by placing your closed fingers two to three inches away from the body and making 10 small, clockwise circles, or by simply visualizing the energy centers as being open.

I would like to share some perspectives to understand our energy centers:

First energy center (root chakra), moves downward and represents your connection to the earth's consciousness, your connection to your physical body, the quantity and quality of your life force, and your physical survival. This is your energetic grounding center; it enables you to be practical mentally and emotionally. The conditions that close this first energy center include being emotionally or mentally burned-out, having fears, being tired, long hours of work, lack of sleep, or holding onto old mind's perspectives that have been passed on to you by your ancestors.

When your energy center is open in a circular moving vertically and counterclockwise about two to four inches in diameter, it implies that you are mentally, physically, and spiritually grounded, practical, and less fearful about life.

Your second back energy center (sacral chakra which is located above the tailbone) represents the strength, quantity, and quality of your sexual energy. When your energy center is open, moving circular and horizontally clockwise along with your heart energy center about two to four inches in diameter, it shows that you are mentally, physically, emotionally, spiritually, and sexually open to your partner.

Having sexual shame, having sex just to please others, or not understanding what love really is, may cause this energy center to close. This may be due to holding onto old ideas about sex passed down to you by your parents and religious institutions.

Your third back energy center (behind your solar plexus) represents your self-healing ability. When this energy center is open, moving circular and horizontally clockwise about two to four inches in diameter, it indicates that you are mentally, emotionally, physically, and spiritually healing yourself.

Consciously or unconsciously choosing to hold back on your self-healing ability or stop taking care of yourself, caused by old mind's perspective stored in your subconscious level closes this energy center.

Your fourth back energy center (behind your heart chakra) represents your true spiritual identity: love. When this energy center is open, moving circularly and horizontally clockwise in a circular motion about two to four inches in diameter, it shows that you are consciously aware of your internal love and ready to express it with others.

Holding back your spiritual identity (love), caused by the old mind's perspective passed down to you, closes this energy center.

The fifth back energy center (behind your neck) represents your personal goals. When this energy center is open moving circularly and horizontally clockwise about two to four inches in diameter, it indicates that you are expressing your passion at work as well as maturing mentally, emotionally, physically, and spiritually.

If your personal goals are not being realized, it is because this energy center is closed, and you may be affected by old ideas passed down to you by your ancestors that are not making you see your purpose in life which is love.

The sixth back energy center (behind your forehead) represents your creativity in your personal and work environments. When this energy center is open, moving circular and horizontally clockwise about two to four inches in diameter, it shows that you are enjoying your work as well as maturing mentally, emotionally, physically, and spiritually.

If you are not enjoying your present work, you will be repressing your creative side, and this energy center will close. If you consciously choose something you love in your work environment, then you will automatically become more creative, and you will keep this energy center open.

Your second front energy center (located below your navel) represents your emotional expression and connection with yourself and others. When this energy center is open, moving circular and horizontally counterclockwise about two to four inches in diameter, it represents your mental, emotional, physical, and spiritual expression.

Consciously or unconsciously choosing to hold back your emotional connection with others, caused by holding onto old ideas, closes this energy center. If you consciously choose to emotionally connect more with others through your spiritual perspectives, then you will keep this energy center open.

Your third front energy center (solar plexus chakra) represents your outlook on life, your self-esteem, and your personal power. When this energy center is open, moving circular and horizontally counterclockwise about two to four inches in diameter, it implies that you are consciously aware of expressing yourself freely.

Feeling guilty or ashamed of yourself for offenses you have given others may close this energy center.

Your fourth front energy center (heart chakra) represents your love relationship and your ability to unconditionally receive, give and accept yourself and others for who they are. When this energy center is open, moving circular and horizontally counterclockwise about two to four inches in diameter, it implies that you are mentally, emotionally, physically, and spiritually nurturing yourself and others.

Consciously or unconsciously choosing to hold back love for yourself and others, caused by old ideas passed down to you, closes this energy center. If this energy center is closed, it indicates that you may feel sadness, isolation, and depression, or are going through hard times in your present relationship.

Your fifth front energy center (throat chakra) represents your feelings, spiritual self-expression, and communication with others. When this energy center is open, moving circular and horizontally counterclockwise about two to four inches in diameter, it suggests that you are mentally, emotionally, physically and spiritually expressing your feelings.

If you keep consciously or unconsciously choosing to hold back on verbally expressing your feelings over the years, this energy center will close, and affect your physical body in areas such as the thyroid. You can express yourself mentally with others, but it is more important to express your feelings, so they know how you feel about them.

Your sixth front energy center (forehead/third eye chakra) represents your spiritual understanding of life. When this energy center is open, moving circularly and horizontally counterclockwise about two to four inches in diameter, it implies that you can see auras and souls in different dimensions.

Holding back your spiritual understanding, caused by the old mind's perspective passed down to you, can close this energy center.

Your seventh energy center (crown chakra/top of your head) moving vertically counterclockwise, represents the knowledge of and connection to your higher consciousness. When this energy center is open in a circular motion about two to four inches in diameter, it suggests the expression of your soul and conscious creative mind.

If you keep consciously or unconsciously choosing to hold back your cosmic connection or understanding, this energy center closes.

Your eighth energy center above your crown chakra represents your participation in global consciousness. This energy center reflects your ability to experience similar thought patterns with others simultaneously or experience telepathic communication. When this energy center is open, moving vertically and counterclockwise about two to four inches in diameter, it indicates that your mind and soul are consciously connected with others.

Repressing your affiliation with group consciousness (Oneness with others), caused by old ideas of separation passed down to you, closes this energy center, as does holding onto negative ideas about others.

The ninth and tenth energy centers are about seven inches above your eighth energy center. They represent your connection to the cosmic inspirations of highly evolved beings and throughout this galaxy. When this energy center is open, moving vertically and counterclockwise about two to four inches in diameter, it indicates that your soul and Spirit have come together to spiritually express and share your inner cosmic wisdom with others.

Other Important Energy Centers

Your chest or breasts energy centers represent self–nurturing or nurturing towards yourself and others at the mental, emotional, physical, and spiritual levels. When the energy center of the right chest or breast is open moving horizontally and clockwise while the energy center of the left chest or breast is moving counterclockwise, this may indicate that they are open and that you are nurturing yourself and others mentally, emotionally, and physically. However, when these energy centers are closed, it may indicate that you are not taking care of yourself. This perspective over the years may cause health challenges to your chest or breasts area.

To open most of the energy centers in your body, use your right or left fingers closed together and make ten small circles going clockwise.

In addition, when one of the energy centers is too open in a circular motion between six to eight inches in diameter, this is an indication that it is expressing an excess of energy or emotion. To balance this energy center, use your fingers closed together and make ten circles horizontally about two to four inches moving clockwise to make the energy center smaller.

Your ears, eyes, mouth, shoulders, elbows, hips, ankles, hands, and feet also have energy centers, and they too can be open or closed.

Some energy centers that are closed can be opened by expanding your mind's perspectives into a more spiritual one. For instance, if you begin to believe that you are a worthy person, then you will become exactly that because it is the natural self of your soul.

FONT & BACK ENERGY CENTERS

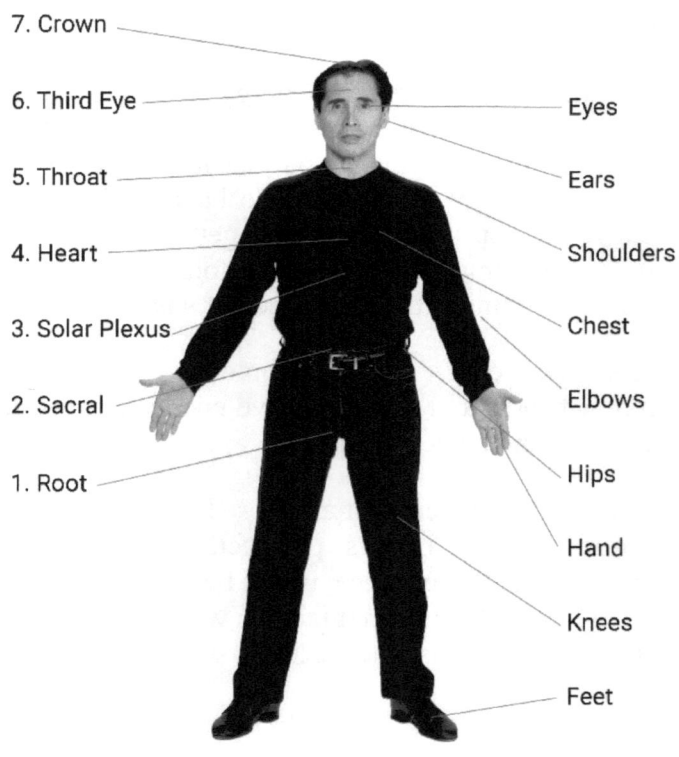

- 7. Crown
- 6. Third Eye
- 5. Throat
- 4. Heart
- 3. Solar Plexus
- 2. Sacral
- 1. Root

- Eyes
- Ears
- Shoulders
- Chest
- Elbows
- Hips
- Hand
- Knees
- Feet

Chapter 20

The Wisdom of Dreams

Dreams are messages from the subconscious mind, spiritual guides, or soul, to guide us and overcome challenges in our daily lives. Dreams can also be thoughts, wishes, and fantasies sent by your loved ones to let you know they are thinking of you.

Some people don't remember their dreams believing they are a function of the brain generating image and opinions in the mind. They may not place importance on dreams or may not be interested in understanding the meanings of them. Furthermore, dreams are interpreted differently in different cultures. But understanding dreams is vital to understanding oneself.

Interpreting dreams, my own as well as those of my friends and clients, have helped me to find some clues and answers to the challenges we are all facing in life. Dreams have been an important tool for me to understand my spirituality. For example, if you are dreaming of flying it indicates that you are rising your spiritual awareness, or if you are having nightmares, it indicates that you are experiencing confusing times with yourself or with others.

I would like to share some brief perspectives and experiences on dreams:

Dreams are out-of-body/astral travel experiences of your soul, which occur during sleep, and sometimes during meditation.

∞

Dreams can be spiritual messages sent from your soul to your conscious creative mind, guiding and helping you solve your personal challenges with others.

∞

Dreams are spiritual realities that can be more important than your physical reality. Your spiritual reality can help you evolve faster at any given moment through your spiritual perspectives when you choose to.

∞

Dreams are information about your present and past life's experiences. Dreams can also be premonitions, thoughts that will soon materialize in physical form. Act on the visions of your dreams. Your positive action now produces your future spiritual experiences.

∞

Dreams bring awareness that changes are on the way. Listen to your dreams. Write down your dreams and watch your life unfold in the manner your dreams have foretold. Nightmares are also dreams letting you know that your life with yourself and others has become dysfunctional.

∞

Dreams can communicate with you in a non-linear way. They are metaphors, which allow you to interpret them according to your mindset or spiritual awareness.

∞

If you just think that dreams can give you constructive messages, but you don't do anything about them, you are not taking advantage of the information. You have the power to change yourself if you choose to.

∞

In dreams, your soul's consciousness communicates through symbols and images to your mind to create a message.

∞

Dreams are multidimensional experiences that allow you to time travel. For instance, as an adult, have you ever dreamt of watching yourself as a young child with your parents or siblings playing together at home? This spiritual experience of time travel through a dream/out-of-body experience can help you transcend your mind and become more aware of your spiritual self. Remember, the past, present, and future are happening simultaneously.

∞

Through lucid dreaming, you can create a spiritual experience with another soul while sleeping. Lucid dreams occur when you wake up in the middle of a dream, go back to sleep, and then consciously return to your dream state and experience the rest of the dream. You can be in control of your lucid dreams and produce your own outcome!

∞

Dreams can be messages of your past lives making you aware of who you were in the past and who you are now in this present life: a more evolved person.

∞

Dreams are a tool to communicate with a loved one who has passed on before you. While living on this earth, you can communicate through your dreams with your loved ones. Before going to sleep, talk to your deceased dad, mom, sister, brother, etc., ask her/him to give you a message through your dreams (an out-of-body experience), and say this three times: "I will remember my dream about dad, mom, sister, etc." You will be surprised that with some practice you will remember your dream and the message the following day.

∞

Dreaming of being insecure or jealous in your intimate relationship is reminding you to work on yourself. This kind of dream can make you lose sleep and become insecure about your partner, or make you consciously aware and overcome your insecurity.

∞

Daydreaming is when someone is imagining, thinking, or having a fantasy about someone or something. Daydreaming may also imply that someone is bored doing things she/he doesn't like or is getting distracted from the past or future. Also, daydreaming and meditating about your personal and spiritual desires can help you achieve them sooner. Daydreaming can be a powerful visualization tool. If you nurture and interpret your daydreams with spiritual awareness, you can materialize and experience your personal desires quickly. On the other hand, daydreaming without action will not help you materialize your dreams.

Chapter 21

Spiritual Healing

The world is slowly changing and moving toward a brighter future. We are becoming more aware of our higher consciousness. This, in turn, will help us make more constructive choices so that our actions will unite us rather than divide us.

Spiritual healing is the awareness and experience of love, joy, and peace within your soul, alleviating your mental, physical, emotional, and spiritual imbalances. Some spiritual healers are becoming more aware of this new higher consciousness and have become more effective healers. When you are feeling good during a spiritual healing session from a healer, she/he is sharing her/his higher energy with you. Feeling good is a spiritual expression of your soul letting you know that you are on the right path.

"Rich in health" is slowly becoming popular in our society because most of us realize that life without good health, no matter how financially wealthy we are, limits our ability to enjoy it. Money can give you physical and mental comfort, but your soul's consciousness can give you great health, and self-confidence, as well as emotional, mental, and spiritual comfort so you can enjoy your life to the fullest.

I have always been fascinated by people's mindset, the soul, emotions, and traits they inherited from their parents. I started working as a spiritual healer and life coach, giving talks on spirituality as well as teaching yoga and writing books. Through my many years of experience I have learned that many people are looking for answers outside of themselves, rather than internally. If we can change our mindset through our soul's consciousness, we can also change our lives.

I would like to share the following spiritual perspectives on spiritual healing that you can use for yourself and others:

A spiritual healer is one who shares and creates energy—healing during a session for someone to give herself/himself the opportunity or chose to heal her/himself.

∞

A spiritual healer needs to ask permission to give healing to the client before a session, to connect and experience unity at the energy level. Healing others without their consent is the work of the mind and false ego and may not work because the client is not ready to be healed through you.

∞

To speed up the healing process of a client, put your mind aside, and allow your soul or wisdom to give you directions. Sometimes when others don't have a desire to be healed, spiritual healing may not work, no matter how hard the healer tries. Remember, self-healing is one's personal decision and desire to become healthy.

∞

Spiritual healing is a multidimensional energy, and it is mindless; that is, it works beyond the mind, allowing you to be in touch with your soul for guidance. When you become aware that all healing methods use higher frequency energy, you can help others heal faster. When you, the healer, are in love with life and with people, then the client's love will be turned on for self-healing to take place at the consciousness or physical level.

∞

Spiritual healing is the process of restoring balance to your conscious mind, body, emotions and spiritual self. When you let go of some of your old mind's perspective passed on to you by your ancestors that have caused imbalances in your outlook, then spiritual healing naturally will take place. When you heal your mind from your old consciousness, you also heal your body at a cellular level. When you believe you are a worthy human being, then your body chemistry at the cellular level will change, and you can become healthier.

∞

When a spiritual healer sees perfection and the magnificent human being the client is, then the healer is inviting the client to experience and co-create her/his own healing process.

∞

Hands-on or hands-off spiritual healing are both effective methods. As the healer, the way you begin to practice with your client depends on what you are comfortable with. Some healers use affirmations for the client to say out loud in order to balance the body chemistry or her/his conscious mind.

∞

Healing others involves holistically working on a client's physical, mental, and emotional aspects, and not just the symptoms of the problems. If the client has a health condition, find out what kind of mindset she/he has before healing sessions to treat the underlying cause, usually by changing an old mindset into a new spiritual perspective.

∞

To protect yourself from a client's negative energy, raise your vibration by embodying love, compassion, joy, peace, and freedom. This spiritual protection will empower your energy.

∞

Sending good vibes to others is another form of spiritual healing that helps them elevate their energy and immune system.

∞

We are all capable of doing our own self-healing, which can be performed with our hands. Using the fingers of your right hand, make ten circles clockwise on your left palm, then do the same with the fingers of your left hand, making ten circles counterclockwise on your right palm. Now, rub your palms together for twenty seconds and place them on the part of the body where you feel discomfort. Do this, two or three times a day until the discomfort goes away.

∞

Self-healing is a form of being peaceful with oneself through meditation because peacefulness elevates your higher consciousness. This in turn affects the mental, physical, emotional, and spiritual states.

∞

Self-healing is the awareness of a new spiritual perspective that comes from your soul into your conscious mind to create health if you choose to.

∞

Sharing laughter with others awakes the joy to heal the conscious mind and body. Laughter opens your heart's energy center, which allows you to become more open-minded to heal yourself. Joy brings healing at the cellular level because you are raising your vibration.

∞

Hugging others is another form of healing. Have you ever felt warm energy while someone is hugging you? If so, this is because you and the other person are sharing each other's self-healing. Hug those who are having challenges in life to comfort them.

∞

Couple dancing is another form of spiritual healing when you dance together. This is because when two people are dancing close together with physical contact they are sharing, exchanging, or feeding each other is energy healing. The more you and your partner dance together the more you will exchange energy at the soul level and become similar in thought pattern.

∞

Since all things have energy and consciousness, you can heal some of your health conditions by drinking a glass of water before meals. Before you drink a glass of filtered water, put the glass close to your mouth and say this affirmation three times a day, "Thank you, water, for making me healthier," or "I love you water." What you are doing is using your thoughts, intentions, and energy to convert the vibration of the conscious water into healing water. You can do the same thing with the foods you eat.

∞

Healing yourself through your spiritual guides is another form of self-healing. By healing yourself and others, you are sending peace and harmony into the world.

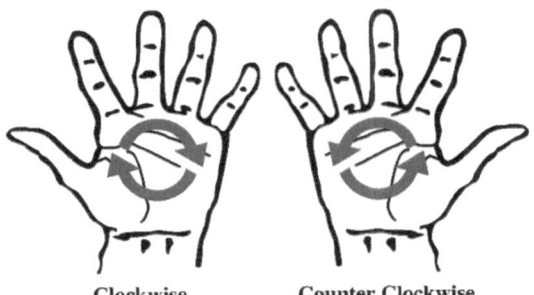

Clockwise　　Counter Clockwise

Energy open

Chapter 22

Healing Experiences

Increasingly, Reiki healing and other types of spiritual healing have become important tools in hospitals and healing centers. Many nurses provide different types of healing energy such as Reiki healing sessions by patient request, as it can speed up the healing process before and after surgery; can trigger a sense of peacefulness after trauma; can help to relieve emotional discomforts such as fear, stress, guilt, grief, depression, and anger.

The more you understand the healing process, the more in touch with your soul you will become. Both the giver and the receiver of a healing session can benefit greatly from the positive energy exchange at the emotional and spiritual level during the healing session.

Experiencing peace in your mind and soul can allow you to live your life more peacefully. Peacefulness can slowly heal your body at the cellular level. When you react negatively to others or to circumstances, you will stop being creative and having more difficulties finding solutions to your challenges.

Below are some of my spiritual healing experiences with my clients:

In 1997 in Washington, DC, I went to a spiritual institute and participated in a healing service. There were two spiritual healers (another person and me) standing about fifteen feet from each other and about six feet away from the audience. The room became quiet, and the pianist played meditation music for the brief healing treatment we were providing to the group. I closed my eyes and opened my palms facing up.

Suddenly, I felt some force simultaneously open both of my hands with my wider palms towards the audience to channel energy. My hands got warmer, and the heat stopped after a few minutes. I wondered who had opened my palms. When I opened my eyes, no one was around me, except the other healer on my left side. I realized and accepted that my spiritual guides were contributing to the healing process we had performed on the audience.

∞

In early 2001, I saw a female client in Washington, DC who called to request a Reiki healing session. I drove her home. It was a messy home, and as I looked for a place between the kitchen and the dining room to put my Reiki table, I wondered if she could afford to pay me for my services. Since I was already there, I decided I would do my best, regardless of payment. I closed my eyes and thanked the Spirit and my soul guides for this opportunity that we created.

A few minutes later, she was lying on my table, and I began the session. Both of my arms, from my triceps all the way down to my hands, began to get hot for what felt like a long time—though it was only about one or two minutes. This was an incredible experience! I felt energy channeling through my arms, helping the client to experience her own self-healing process and balance her old mindset, which had been producing mental, emotional, and physical disharmony.

I had not experienced this intensity of energy before. I was aware, through the energy flow, that she had not been able to express herself verbally, that she was afraid of life, that she was not able to connect emotionally with others, and most importantly, that she didn't know about spirituality. After thirty minutes, I finished the session and gave her a life coaching session and suggestions on how to understand her spiritual life.

After the session, my client, formerly confused and upset, now felt emotionally and mentally balanced, calm, centered, and alert. A few minutes later she went to the kitchen, reached for her purse, and paid for the session. I hesitated and asked, "Are you sure?" "Yes," she said, "I feel better."

∞

In 2004, the brother of my babysitter from Lima, Peru, asked me for spiritual healing for swelling in his face. I agreed and asked for his permission to perform the healing. He accepted. I asked him to give me a recent picture of himself so he could rest at home while I remotely sent him energy healing before his bedtime. Pictures of people are connected to them at the energy level, regardless of how far away they may be. I wrote his full name and address on the back of the photo, held it in both my hands and on my heart, and sent him a healing for twenty minutes. One hour later he reported that the swelling in his face was reduced by 90 percent.

∞

In 2011, a friend of mine, a former clinical psychologist, came to my home in Potomac, Maryland for a Reiki session. This was his experience in his own words:

It happened during a Reiki healing session with Carlos Gutierrez, a longtime friend. I was lying on my back on a table during the healing session and at the end, he let me rest a few moments, then said, "You can get up now." I heard him say this, and began to rouse myself to sit up. I slowly began to lift my body to a seated position on the table with my legs dangling over the side of the table, when I noticed that I was sitting up, but my body was not! It was a very odd experience, sitting there looking down at myself. Then I noticed that another me was lying on the table and started to repeat the motion to sit up, but it was like a series of photographs of someone moving.

Chapter 23

The New Holistic Life Coach

A professional spiritual life coach can help you speed up the process of your growth, health, and love relationship by helping you remember who you are spiritually and changing your old perspective into a new one.

We have been spiritually repressed, which has led us to impatient, unhealthy, and dysfunctional relationships. However, as we are becoming more aware of transitions in spiritual consciousness in our world, we can attain new consciousness to improve our lives all around.

I would like to share some brief perspectives on spiritual life coaching to improve your life:

Spiritual life coaches encourage their clients to feel good about themselves through spiritual perspectives, reminding them to express their love, joy, peace, compassion, and optimism for self-healing to create harmony.

∞

An experienced spiritual life coach is one who gives spiritual perspectives to help the client understand the fears that they have learned through their parents and religious institutions. If they understand what causes their fears, then they can overcome them.

∞

When you find a spiritual life coach, do a couple of sessions before committing to short or long-term treatments. It is important to note how comfortable you feel with her/him before deciding how many sessions you may need. If you feel internally comfortable with your life coach, then you can speed up your own healing process.

You, the client, may feel more comfortable doing a session in person with a spiritual life coach. However, doing it virtually, may also be helpful.

∞

An experienced life coach who does spiritual healing can help you achieve balance by opening your energy centers and releasing stress, traumas, and repressed emotions that you may have been holding onto. After a session, she/he can advise you on how to transcend your spiritual perspective to overcome personal challenges.

∞

All healing sessions are an exchange of the soul's energies between clients, spiritual guides, and the healer.

Chapter 24

Your Health

Health is the balance between the mind, body, emotions, and soul. When you are spiritually evolving, you can create the opportunity to be naturally healthy at the mental, emotional, physical, and spiritual levels. It is important to understand that some physical and mental health challenges begin at the thought level or can be something you have inherited from your parents, such as a heart condition, diabetes, alcoholism, etc.

This does not necessarily mean you are going to experience your parents' health conditions, but you may be prone to have similar health issues as them if you don't take care of yourself. If you change the way you think about yourself, you can change your life.

I would like to share some perceptions on health to improve your life:

Your health is an expression of your conscious mind. Your body is listening to you when you are experiencing stress, fear, violence, depression, anxiety, or low self-esteem affecting the body. If you keep consciously or unconsciously experiencing these emotional states over the years, you can lower your immune system and develop diseases. By feeling happy, confident, optimistic, loving, being mentally, emotional, and physically active, on the other hand, you can raise your immune system and stay healthy.

When you repress your mental, emotional, and spiritual aspects over the years, it can create stress, inflammation, and sickness in your physical body.

∞

Your physical body is an expression of your mind and soul's consciousness, which carries your present and old mind's perspective that can serve or harm your body. Your soul transports your physical body. Without your soul, your physical body cannot live.

∞

Being nearsighted may indicate that you focus more on the outside world than on your inner self. You enjoy helping others more than helping yourself. Focusing more on your inner world may encourage you to achieve internal balance.

Being farsighted may demonstrate that you focus more on your inner self than the outside world. You enjoy helping yourself more than helping others. Focusing more on the outside world may help you stimulate balance.

∞

Headaches may indicate stress/tension/negativity at the energy level you are putting on yourself. Headaches are often caused by holding onto distorted negative thoughts because they drain your energy level.

∞

Obesity may be inherited or caused by a poor diet or consuming unhealthy processed foods or many animal products over the years. Being obese can make it challenging for the soul to carry your physical body, and as a result, you may become immobile. Changing your eating habits and doing blood tests for food allergies may be recommended to improve your health.

∞

If you have challenges staying healthy, you can be discouraged from evolving spiritually. But being healthy doesn't need to be a challenge; a simple, natural diet can be easy and affordable for many people. Taking time to prepare or cook your healthy food can be inexpensive. Drinking plain or filtered water is more beneficial than drinking carbonated sodas or tap water full of chemicals.

∞

Daily exercise such as doing gentle yoga, running, dancing, walking, lifting weights, or swimming can be incorporated into your health regimen. Keeping yourself mentally and physically in good shape will make you feel better about yourself.

∞

Words are powerful tools. They condition your mind, generate your opinions, influence your behavior, change your body chemistry, and affect your immune system. Verbally expressing negative and pessimistic thoughts lowers your energy and your immune system, which can eventually affect your health. Expressing bad words or cursing has negative energy that keeps feeding into your physical body. Constructive words have more optimistic energy that can bring balance to your health.

Chapter 25

Our Inevitable Transition and Reincarnation

What is passing away, and where do we go after this life? Many people believe in some form of life after death. It is important to understand that we don't die spiritually because the soul lives forever, and our physical body is a temporary tool that our soul expresses through love.

When we pass away, we change from our physical state to the spiritual one, and we will remain within these multidimensional fields here and now to meet our family members, loved ones, and friends who passed on before us.

I would like to share a few perspectives about death and reincarnation to stop you fearing death:

The passing of a loved one can be tragic or traumatic if we don't understand how our spiritual lives work. You cannot ever die spiritually at the soul level because we are all eternal, spiritual beings living in different dimensions simultaneously. You may feel that passing away of a loved one is tragic because you have learned that death is the end of life, so death may be what you fear most in life.

The passing of a loved one only means you stop seeing her/him physically, but not spiritually. We are all still living here together but in different dimensions. Sometimes, while you are sleeping, you can see the soul of a loved one or feel her/his presence. They come and visit during your sleep to comfort you in times of need.

When you pass away from this physical world, you bring the essence of your soul, which is unconditional love, into heaven and leave the residues (positive and negative energies-part of your soul) in this physical plane as a ghost.

∞

Suffering because of the passing of a loved one is the reaction of your old perception and an interpretation of death through the mind's limited spiritual perspective. You have learned to grieve the death of your loved one instead of celebrating the soul's departure to another journey in heaven.

∞

Passing (crossing over) is your soul entering into another spiritual dimension within this physical dimension, right here, right now. When you are taking your last breath, your loved ones who have passed on before you will be waiting for you, cheering you on and welcoming you to your new life.

∞

Celebrate the passing of your loved ones: it is the special spiritual journey into a new life that your soul has. If you have mentally and emotionally suffered from your parents' deaths, do you want your children to suffer from your passing? If the answer is no, then give them spiritual education to ease the suffering for when you pass, so they can celebrate your departure.

∞

To pass away is to awaken from a dream in another dimension and meet your loved ones who have passed away before you. You will continue to reincarnate usually with the same family's group of consciousness here on earth, so you can continue evolving.

∞

The passing is the soul's transition from one state of consciousness to another, an awakening from your own physical illusion.

∞

The passing is the soul saying goodbye to your old mind's perspective and welcoming your spiritual one. There is no such thing as resting in peace after you "physically pass away" into another dimension and continue to live spiritually at the soul level.

After you have passed on the residue of your soul's energy will remain in this physical dimension to comfort the loved ones within their soul from their mental suffering.

∞

A "natural" passing is when someone passes on without any mental and physical struggle during sleep. It also occurs when no one is around.

∞

There is no such thing as a "lost soul" in this universe. All souls go to heaven here and now within this dimension and later come back to earth or another planet within this galaxy again to evolve in consciousness and help others.

∞

When you pass away, you will bring your true personality into heaven and realize who you really are: love. Similarly, if you are emotionally, physically, or mentally attached to a loved one or material things here on earth, part of your soul will remain here in this dimension of physical reality. When you come back or reincarnate you will bring similar personality traits again.

∞

Suicide is the act of causing one's own death. Catalysts for suicide may include emotional trauma, physical pain, fears, guilt, shame, or depression. Contemplating suicide is a sign that distorted ideas about life have lowered a person's desire to live. Losing your desire to live contributes to death in a hundred different ways such as taking drugs, drinking alcohol, smoking cigarettes, a poor diet, etc.

A spiritual perspective can encourage everyone to improve their desire to live, to stop feeling suicidal and begin to live life more constructively and spiritually. The loved ones who have passed on before us don't want us to suffer; they want us to evolve in consciousness and celebrate life.

∞

A near-death experience (NDE) is your soul leaving your physical body temporarily but not becoming completely disconnected from your physical body. It is your soul giving you, through your conscious mind, the spiritual awareness of life continuing after death. This spiritual awareness can transcend your consciousness and experiences in the physical form. People who have (NDE) experience lose the fear of dying.

An NDE may be caused by an accident, surgery, illness, or suicidal act. During an NDE, you may have an out-of-body experience, seeing your own physical body from above. You may see loved ones or close friends who have passed away before you. They may tell you to return to your physical body, to revolutionize your old ideas and to evolve spiritually. After an NDE, you will become more spiritual, compassionate, helpful, tolerant, unconditionally loving, and less materialistic and fearful about life.

∞

In 1972 my sister's son, Juan Pablo, told me that when he was young, he saw his grandfather passing away, and this is his story:

When I was about six, I was close to my grandfather. He was loving, affectionate, and tolerant of me. When I was young, I didn't understand the concept of death, though I believed in the continuity of life after death. Later in life, my grandfather taught me about death. When I was a teenager, one Sunday afternoon my grandfather was ill, and he went to the hospital, and my parents took me to visit him. I remember the intense color of that Sunday afternoon, and as it turned out, it was going to be a memorable day. At one point my parents left the room and I stayed alone with my grandfather. He was lying down and resting, and I, like any curious teen, was checking out the surroundings. I was watching him, and it seemed that he had fallen asleep.

Suddenly, I saw a vaporous cloud coming out of the top of his head, like steam coming out of a kettle but less intensely, more slowly, and noiselessly. I ran to tell my parents that smoke was coming out of the top of my grandfather's head. My parents thought I was kidding but went into the room, only to find out he had passed away. To this day, I recognize how profound it was to have witnessed the moment of grandfather's peaceful passing.

Reincarnation

Reincarnation is the return of your soul into a physical body here on earth or another world within this galaxy to continue to evolve in consciousness no matter who you were in the past. You bring your talents whether in sports, art, dance, acting, business acumen, or medicine from a previous life when you reincarnate in this physical form, doing the same thing because that is what you will remember the most. When you reincarnate into this physical reality, you choose your parents, place, race, gender, birth order and time. Sometimes when we come back on this earth and keep choosing the same father, mother, and we have the same brothers and sisters until we become spiritually evolved and move on through other, more families.

∞

Abortion is a brief lifetime reincarnation in this physical world by the soul of a child. Miscarriage is another type of a short lifetime reincarnation in this physical form created by the unborn baby's soul to bring spiritual awareness to the family or parents.

∞

If you were an evolved soul in a past life time, this you will remember when you reincarnate in this physical world. Thus, you can continue to keep evolving in consciousness and helping others. The less evolved you were in your past life, the less you will remember who you were, so you recreate a new you.

∞

When you and your loved one reincarnate in this physical, it is because you both have decided to come back together through different families to love each other again.

∞

My friend, Martha, has a granddaughter named Lucy. Martha noticed that this child had an excellent memory of her childhood. One day Martha asked, "How far back in your childhood can you remember?" Lucy said, "Grandma, I remember choosing my mother before I was born. I knew I would stay with her and not with my father when they got divorced." In other words, Lucy's soul saw the future of his parents' divorce before she was born and decided to stay with her mom. Such insights are common in children, for their young minds are yet unaffected by the tribulations of life. If you become like a child, quiet your mind, and simplify your thoughts, you, too, will be able to direct your mind to the experiences of your soul before your birth.

∞

Every reincarnation into this physical world is an opportunity to keep spiritually evolving. Keeping this in mind will allow you to have the courage to grow and help others.

Chapter 26

Our Conventional Music

Music is the international language of all cultures. Throughout time, humankind has celebrated its joy, sorrows, pain, and suffering through music and song. Songwriters in all societies write music and lyrics that reflect their emotions and world views. Contemporary music of all cultures is a universal language that triggers deep love or fear.

Listening to intense music with sad and painful lyrics can lower your mood. Listening to romantic, happy, and playful music with upbeat lyrics can freshen your mood and inspire you to dance and celebrate life.

I would like to share some perceptions about music so you can choose the music you want to express, sing, or dance:

All music radiates vibration/frequency that can help complement your energy flow or disrupt it. For example, unbearably loud music or songs such as heavy metal or distorted sounds can lower your positive energy level and make you feel very tense or make you angry, as though someone is complaining and screaming at you. Conversely, listening to slow and soothing instrumental music can make you feel more relaxed and comfortable.

∞

Music is energy that creates vibrations that can be positive or negative. It can trigger subconscious memories and stimulate happiness or sadness, pain or healing, trauma, or peace. Music that triggers joy and good memories makes your heart and soul ascend. Music that reminds you of pain, sorrows, breakups, anger, revenge, and dramas can trigger and bring back difficult memories and eventually can make you feel sick or stressed.

∞

The sound of violent or horror movies can affect your body at the cellular level. Your body is listening to and feeling everything you experience in your life, and since your mind doesn't know of what is real and what it is not it can affect you at the mental, emotional, and spiritual level. For instance, when your body is listening to and watching horror movies, your body will react and trigger the fear that can affect your health in the long run.

∞

Music created from love carries a higher vibrations and healing energy. This restores the listener at the cellular level. Happy music is a form of healing. It temporarily balances your mind, body, emotions, and soul.

∞

Music brings people together to celebrate life and unity. Anyone can dance to any music with anyone. Dance is the universal language that communicates with dancers through music.

∞

Listening to a variety of music implies that you have a flexible personality and an open, expansive mind. Choosing happy music will make you feel good about yourself!

∞

Stop listening to love songs that express drama, need, expectation, dependency, depression, and dysfunctional relationships among ourselves to keep us reminding us of our insecurities and fears. If we want to evolve into higher consciousness, listen to music to a more optimistic outlook to help us overcome our personal challenges.

∞

Here are some music lyrics that may trigger fears and cause you to keep reliving your past negative experiences:

"I am lost without you."
"I need your love."
"You belong to me."
"I am nothing without you."
"You are everything to me."
"Me and my broken heart."

Continuing to listen to music with these kinds of lyrics may convince you that you are not in control of your life. It may cause you to repress your spirituality and validate your mental and emotional suffering/lower consciousness, which are old ideas passed down to you by your society or your culture.

∞

Singing happy songs allows you to attract and create joyful circumstances. Write and sing happy music inspired by love to heal our world. Write spiritual music to lift our souls. Sing happy songs and you will attract happiness:

"I love myself!"
"I love but I don't need you."
"I am perfect".
"I found myself though you."
"No more wars."
"Unity is the answer."

Chapter 27

Some of My Spiritual Revelations and Experiences

Throughout my life, I always had one foot in my spiritual reality and the other in my physical reality. I have had many physical reincarnations, I continue to have experiences of heightened personal spiritual awareness and amazing encounters with evolved souls and evolved beings within this galaxy. My journey with my soul's spiritual experiences began when I was a baby. I am the fourth child of six siblings and was reincarnated on Earth on the mountain of Matucana, two hours from the city of Lima, Peru.

As a child, I was acutely aware of the spiritual world and the spontaneous manifestations of souls. I saw people's auras, sensed people's intentions, and saw ghosts and souls. Sometimes, I could hear my soul vibrating so fast it sounded like a flying bee. I was attracted to or created these spiritual experiences; they happened automatically and intuitively. I came to understand that for me, this was natural, but kept it to myself. Subconsciously, I knew my family would not understand.

When I was a child, I couldn't speak until I was six years old because I was so involved with my spiritual experiences such as out-of-body experiences (astral projections) and seeing souls in the upper corner of my bedroom. I didn't know what any of these experiences meant. Later, I became aware that ever since I was a child my family, neighbors, and friends had been taking care of me so later I could become a spiritual messenger.

At the age of seven, I became aware and felt that my parents adopted me in this physical form when I was born through them. We are all adopted children by our parents in this physical world because we are coming through them.

I would like to share some of my spiritual experiences about my life that made me eventually a spiritual messenger:

Coming to Earth from within this Galaxy

I had my first deep spiritual vision when I was four. I was in my bedroom alone at bedtime wondering about life. My eyes were closed, and suddenly, through my third eye, I saw my white-colored soul coming to Earth. At that moment, I understood that my soul had formerly
reincarnated in many places as an ascendent galactic soul traveler life coach through different races within this galaxy such as Syrians, Pleiadians, Sumerians, and now as a human. We are all coming from different place within this galaxy.

At the time, I didn't imagine that I might have been a being from another world or another race; I thought my family and I were just people like everybody else. I know now that my soul came with a purpose: to share its wisdom, love, and compassion. It makes sense now. But then, at the age of four, everything was a mystery to me.

Later that same year, I wondered what my future held. For the first time, I heard my spiritual inner voice say, "You are going to be fine in life." I stopped being concerned about what was happening and began to trust my inner voice. And indeed, I have done well most of my life.

My intuition has been a touchstone for me. I have always relied on it and allowed it to lead me along an increasingly lucid spiritual path. I have grown and become a spiritual life coach as a result. Because I had faith that my intuition would not let me down, I was able to share intuitive metaphysical (cause and effect/beyond physical) psychology, spiritual healing, and spiritual experiences with my social and career circles for the betterment of all.

All manner of spiritual phenomena occurred when I was a boy, but I didn't realize how different I was. For example, imagine my surprise as a small child when I suddenly felt the presence of little souls (little round light bulbs) hovering around adult women who came to our home. Later, I discovered that some of these women friends became pregnant.

When I was eight, I became aware of my internal spiritual perspective: I understood the spiritual truth about eternal life and reincarnation. I began to sense with my third eye souls and ghosts and concluded that passing away was merely physical, not spiritual—that we simply change form by leaving our physical bodies to return to the spiritual universe (heaven within this dimension) until our next physical journey or reincarnation.

Over time, I became aware that I could see my aura, or soul, through my third eye in the form of magenta-colored energy in front of me when I closed my eyes during my meditation. I also came to understand that I came to Earth of my own free will to keep evolving into higher consciousness by helping others become aware of their spiritual lives.

Early Experiences with Ghosts

When I was ten, I was taking a nap while my younger brother was in the next bed, when suddenly, I felt invisible negative energy (lower consciousness) push into my solar plexus. I became physically and mentally paralyzed; I couldn't talk or move a muscle. I mentally called out to my brother to help me but he couldn't hear me. I had never experienced anything so strange. I was afraid. My mother had told me months before that if ghosts ever bothered me, to fight back, get angry, and curse them. I tried that, and it worked. After a few minutes of struggling with this negative ghost, it went away.

Years later, I had another negative ghost encounter. I was picking up my parents in my car for a trip to the grocery store and I was parked outside their front lobby waiting, when suddenly I felt my third-eye opening, tingling between my eyebrows. Suddenly, I saw a man on the right side pointing a pistol at my head. Scared, I quickly move my head backwards, then realized that it was just a ghost who wanted to scare me. It succeeded!

UFO Encounter

When I was fourteen, I saw a UFO (unidentified flying object) for the first time in Lima. It was one of the most exciting experiences I have ever had. I could relate it to things I already suspected about life, things I had known intuitively about other beings from other galaxies.

It was early on a winter evening. I was alone in my parents' bedroom, staring out at my neighbor's window. I looked up and saw a big, dark, oval object with flashing white lights flying above the roof of our townhouse. I ran up to the third floor and watched it from more less thirty feet away from me, as it slowly and silently lifted away and disappeared into the sky. I kept the experience to myself. Much later, when I told my parents about it, my mother didn't believe me.

My Inner Voice Experience

In 1980's I was living in Arlington, Virginia US. I had another supernatural experience. I was lying down with my eyes closed. I woke up suddenly when the outside noises stopped, I hear a gentle waterfall in the lower back of my head. A clear voice said to me, "Don't be afraid." Nothing more. The voice was neither male nor female, just a beautiful voice communicating with me…. "Don't be afraid." Notwithstanding these words of assurance, I was frightened, so I opened my eyes and said, "Who's there?" But there was no answer. I realized then and there that my inner voice, or spiritual guide, was introducing herself/himself.

Later, in my parents' apartment, I was meditating on my bed with my eyes closed. After a few minutes, my third-eye opened, and I saw a white-colored soul on the ceiling pointing its hands towards me. My soul lifted suddenly from my physical body, and I flew up to the ceiling. As I floated around, I felt so good, so light, rejuvenated, and peaceful. After a few seconds my soul descended, returning to my physical body and I opened my eyes and exclaimed, "Awesome!"

Seeing My Children's Souls for the First Time

In 1981's an intuitive friend told me that soon I was going to meet a woman who would be very important in my life. I sensed this as a real possibility. Two months later, a new dance student joined my salsa class in Bethesda, Maryland and, weeks later, we started dating. A few months later, she invited me to her home. We were lying down on the sofa and kissing when suddenly I saw two souls above my left side (round and white, about four inches in diameter) descend from the eight-foot ceiling towards her upper body. Then, I heard my inner voice say, "You will have two children with this woman."

A year later my girlfriend and I were married. Five years later, our first daughter was born. Two years after that, our second daughter arrived. I enjoyed being a dad, and I had a lot of fun with my kids before they went to college in Canada. Now they are studying: the older one in her third year of medical school (also studying holistic medicine) in St Louis Missouri, and the younger one in her first year doing master's degree on International Relations in Geneva, Switzerland.

Experiences with Ghosts

In 1983 my wife and I were teaching dancing at Gettysburg College in Pennsylvania. We checked into the hotel nearby and went to sleep at 11:00 p.m. Around 3:00 a.m. I began to hear people screaming in the streets; the hotel room phone was ringing, and the

TV started turning on and off by itself. The next day I asked the front desk's clerk if someone had called my room the previous night; the clerk replied, "We didn't call you."

Later, after we taught the dance class, someone told me that the area where we were teaching was the field of the Civil War Battle of Gettysburg. Then I realized that many soldiers in this war had suffered great pain, fear, violence, and many has died; and many had left these negative experiences in the field at the energy level. My intuition was open, and I was able to hear the screaming and suffering of these soldiers who had passed on in the war. But my wife didn't hear anything except the TV turning on and off and the phone ringing.

My Nirvana Experience

In 1987 I became infatuated with my spirituality. I had been aware of the spiritual concept of Nirvana as life's greatest love and highest consciousness when I was younger, but it was not until my thirties that I experienced it.

One day my girlfriend and I were making love, and later my sexual orgasm, my love energy, began to stretch through my upper body's energy opening—it felt so great and tangible. My upper body started shaking back and forth; and then a spiritual awareness came into my conscious mind saying, this is Nirvana.

I realize now that all those years experiencing myself spiritually and knowing myself, helping myself, loving myself, embracing myself, had made me a spiritual messenger.

I have given many talks on spirituality and metaphysics at different spiritual institutes around my area, such as the Metaphysical Chapel and the Institute for Spiritual Development. I have also spoken in Washington, DC, Virginia, Maryland, other U.S. states, and thirty-six countries.

In 1992 I was in my home doing my hour-long daily meditation when suddenly my soul left my body and floated into a silent spiritual dimension. I felt my soul vibrating quickly; it sounded like a flying bee. Suddenly, I felt the uncomfortable presence of a ghost or soul around me. In my mind, I said, "Get out of here!"

Seconds later, as I started naturally floating via astral projection through a mist in the direction of my office, I saw the ghosts of three children (two little girls and a boy). I could see them in their human form at the energy level, and the boy had blood on his right cheek. He was shy and retreated behind my desk when I approached him. Meanwhile, the girls and I were staring at and observing each other.

I decided to go back, and my soul floated towards the recreation room of my home and return to my physical body. I wondered if these children might have once passed away in my house or in my neighborhood. Subsequently, I researched the history of the previous occupants of my home but after several hours of research, I came up empty-handed.

Experiences with Evolved Souls

In 1995 I lived in Falls Church, Virginia in United States. I had been practicing daily meditation to tune into the spirit world. I was lying on my back in my bedroom, meditating, when suddenly I felt my third eye automatically open. I saw dark-colored energy, or soul, in human form with small, bright white lights inside of it sitting on my stomach. We stared at each other, and I felt a distinct female energy. I was amazed but comfortable and unafraid. I sensed that she was from another world or another race in this galaxy or from another dimension. Ten seconds later—she dematerialized and disappeared. I believe she came to validate my perspective of the existence of other spiritual beings throughout this galaxy.

In 1999 I was fascinated by and aware of friendly souls around me helping with my spiritual development. One day, I was meditating in my home when suddenly I experienced an out-of-body/astral projection. An angelic female soul got behind me and held my left hand with her left hand. I held her right hand with my right hand, and our souls flew above the streets of my neighborhood, behind cars and over the sidewalks. Everything was silent.

We flew so high that I could see landmarks from about three thousand feet above the ground. I felt so good, so free, and so protected! I telepathically asked her name, to which she replied, "I am Karla." I started thinking, Yeah, right! What a coincidence! My name is Carlos! I realized right then that she could read my thoughts and I felt embarrassed. But she didn't seem to mind. It felt so good flying around with this female angelic soul. When I saw the sun in front of me I returned to my physical body.

Seeing a Blue Planet

In 2002 I was sitting down on my sofa meditating when suddenly my soul left my physical body and, seconds later, I was floating a thousand miles away in front of a big beautiful light blue planet. It was so amazing! I could see the whole light blue, round planet! Seconds later! I came back to my physical body, amazed by my experience.

Transporting My Soul into Another World

In 2005 after taking my kids to school, I came home and lay down on my bed. Intending to meditate for thirty minutes, I put a pillow over my face. Suddenly someone or something transported my soul into another spiritual dimension; because of my pillow I couldn't see who or what was pulling me out of my body.

Before I can remove my pillow I telepathically heard the voice of an evolved soul saying, "You wanted to know life in other places in this galaxy?" I replied, "Yes." I relaxed, heard a buzzing sound and a bell, and saw a series of concentric circles becoming increasingly smaller and moved into the center of a light that pulled me straight up into another dimension world within this galaxy.

During this transition, I didn't hear a sound or see anything; the light took me into another world. Seconds later, I was in a house, and I saw a friendly man in human form with an orange face and white hair sitting at a desk. I saw my soul floating towards him, and he said telepathically, "Hello, how can I help you?" Seconds later, two females, each with the same-colored skin and physical form, walked into the house while the man and I were standing in. The man then said to me, "Follow me!"

On my way out, I tripped over a table. The two women behind me noticed and acknowledged my soul as a stranger in the house. My soul continued to follow the man, and as I floated through his beautiful yellow garden of glowing bright yellow grass, the grass acknowledged my soul's presence by becoming even shinier.

The man stopped me and pointed to a high place on the ground and said, "Go to the high land to go back home to your world!" The place was a vortex to a different spiritual dimension where one could travel throughout this galaxy. Twice I asked him, "Where am I?" But he didn't answer. Suddenly I returned to my physical body. As I reflected on the experience, I felt relieved that most of my life has been aware of astral travel, out-of-body experiences, and life on other worlds. This out-of-body experience in another world allowed me to understand the nature of my soul.

Meeting with My Sister's and My Dad's Souls

In 2018 my older sister, Maria, passed away from pancreatic cancer. Two hours later, my siblings and I were talking in the living room of my deceased sister's home, when suddenly there was a clear knocking at the front door. One of us opened the door but there was no one there. I believe Maria was knocking at the door to let us know that she was there with us in spirit and was doing fine.

Several months later, as I was meditating I felt myself leave my body and float upwards towards the ceiling of my office. I saw her soul and we hugged each other. With her Spanish sense of humor she said to me telepathically, "You feel like a firewood." She was telling me that to her my soul felt hot. I said to her, "I love you!" Then, seconds later, she left.

Two months later my father had a vivid dream about my sister Maria. She had come to visit him, too, although he had no knowledge of her death. A week later my dad passed away at the age of 97.

In 2020 I was meditating when the residues of my dad's soul sneaked behind my back and asked "What is my last name?" I felt that he was angry with me, and I said, "Gutierrez." A few weeks later, I realized that my dad was not too happy because I was writing my fourth book and I was not going to use his last name, just my first name. He was always very proud of his last name. Later, by the advice of my two editors, I decided to use my last name on my book.

My Former Alien Life Incarnation

In 1983 I drew the picture below. I entered a period of personal introspection wondering about myself, others, life, and where I came from. Later that year, I drew by heart/memory my spiritual self-identity or my former physical incarnation as an evolved being before I came to Earth.

My Spiritual Self-Identity (1983)

Drawing Interpretation One of My Past Life Incarnation

Pencil Drawing by the Author

The oval figure on the top-left of the drawing is a portal into another dimension within a galaxy.

My white-colored soul is on the top-right of the drawing coming and incarnating to Earth from another world. Making the number four with my leg represents the fourth child of my family.

The horizontal number eight above the scale represents infinity, manifestation, and abundance of life.

The short evolved being representing me on the right side of the drawing is holding the balance representing harmony. On the back of my neck is a small evolved being representing my spiritual wisdom, intuition, and ability to share spiritual truths with others.

The tall evolved being on the right side of the drawing represents my higher self (soul), making me aware of life in other worlds. Behind my legs an evolved being holds a ball representing my joyfulness.

The pyramid below the scale represents the balance of my soul, mind, and body.

The number nine (head) on the bottom center of the drawing represents completion in this physical form.

The wheel of life/cycles on the lower-bottom-right of the drawing represents my higher consciousness.

Chapter 28

The Physical Body

The physical body is your vehicle and instrument for the expression of your soul: it holds the and expresses who you are spiritually. You express your spiritual self and display your mental and emotional characteristics based on your perception of yourself.

As you spiritually understand more about your body's consciousness and connection to your mind and soul, you realize you have a thinking body that listens to your mind, especially your subconscious mind.

If you keep consciously or unconsciously choosing to be angry, sad, anxious, or frustrated, your body will respond over time by manifesting these emotions and eventually become ill. However, if you keep consciously or unconsciously choosing to be happy, strong, healthy, and physically active, your body will listen and you can become healthy.

Your soul's consciousness is responsible for the functionality and expression of your physical body.

Your actions and your body language speak louder than words. Body language is the reflection of your thoughts, emotions, and desires at the subconscious level. Ninety percent of communication is through body language. Just ten percent of communication is verbal. To be healthy and happy allow your mind and body to convey your most positive self.

When I was fourteen years of age, I intuitively knew some ideas about the psychological aspects of people's body shapes and body language, including my own. In 1977 I moved from Lima, Peru to the Washington, DC area United States, where I started to observe people's body shapes and body language and the relationship to their mental and emotional characteristics. I began to test this information on friends and acquaintances and, over time, almost always validated my perceptions most of the time.

In 1978 I became a professional ballroom dance instructor, spiritual life coach, and spiritual Reiki healer. I started using my abilities to read people's mental and emotional expressions through their physical shapes and body language. I shared my spiritual perspectives and experiences in my first book in 2002, *The Body Language of Dance*. I use this awareness and experience to help my friends, dance students, and spiritual life coaching clients become more aware of their mental state.

I would like to share some characteristics of the body language and some brief psychological perspectives about the physical body so you can become conscious of what you are revealing. However, people are different and unique at the mental, physical, and emotional level and thus may not apply to everyone of these physical traits and body language characteristics mentioned below:

Tilting your head slightly towards your right side indicates right-brain dominance. Leaning your head towards your left side implies left-brain predominance.

Temple

A small swollen temple implies that you can be short-tempered or that you can easily react negatively to others when things are not working well for you. However, making decisions from your present moment, however, can produce more positive outcomes.

Eyes and Eyebrows

Eyebrows express how you feel about yourself and others. Bushy eyebrows may indicate emotional barriers or that you are overprotective. Scant eyebrows show emotional sensitivity. Having high-set eyebrows implies that you may be short-tempered or react negatively towards others or that you are defensive.

Your eyes are the windows and the expression of your emotions. They express your joy, grief, anger, love, or uncertainties. All your thoughts and emotions create your eyes' expressions.

Protruding or watery eyes imply someone who is emotionally fragile or insecure. Building your spiritual self-confidence can help you become mentally and emotionally stronger.

Deep-set eyes imply being mentally and emotionally grounded; and, for the most part, indicates self-confidence.

Direct, tense, unblinking eye contact may indicate a confrontational and aggressive personality. On the hand, glancing down or making little eye contact with others, shows low self-esteem or lack of self- identity.

Some cultures by custom maintain respect for the elders by looking down while speaking with them. When you connect with others through soft eye contact, then you are connecting with your heart and compassion.

Chin

Holding your chin up and maintaining a soft, friendly facial expression is an indication of self-confidence. On the other hand, holding your chin up with an unfriendly facial expression, implies that you may have a superiority complex and that there is something you don't like about others.

Forehead

A protruding forehead indicates that you may be mentally, emotionally, and physically hard on yourself and others; the accumulation of tension can create puffiness. Lower your expectations and complaints towards others can help you to be more accepting. If you keep consciously or unconsciously choosing to frown, this indicates that you are being angry about someone or something.

Nose

The shape of your nose may show your personality characteristics. A nose tip that goes up may imply you have low self-esteem, no being impatient with yourself and others, or maybe think a lot. A nose tip pointing down toward the lips may indicates down to earth or have a self-centered personality that can be positive or negative.

Lips

Having large lips shows that people are verbally expressive and passionate, while having thin lips may imply that people can express little of their emotions or true feelings. People who have an upper lip larger than their lower lip may hold back sharing material things with others than their loved ones. Those who have a larger lower lip than their upper lip indicate that they like to share with their loved ones and acquaintances alike.

Mouth

If the corners of someone's mouth curl, it may indicate that she/he is joyous and optimistic most of the time, while if she/he has their corners of the mouth pointing downwards, it may show that she/he likes to complain (habit). A protruding mouth implies assertiveness and is verbally aggressive with others.

Voice

Men with feminine voices have right-brain characteristics and may exhibit feminine behavior, a natural ability to attract more female than male friends, and may look physically younger than their age. Women with masculine voices have left-brain characteristics and may exhibit tomboyish behavior. They attract more male than female friends and may look physically older than their age.

Neck

People with long, thin necks are emotionally sensitive and think a lot. Their feelings can easily be hurt. A thick neck, on the other hand, indicates emotional resilience. They are grounded, practical, and easygoing. A protrusion at the back of the neck indicates that a person may be repressing her/his personal goals (positive expectations) or spiritual growth and consciously or unconsciously choosing to help others before helping herself/himself. A protruding Adam's apple shows that an individual may not readily admit her/his mistakes.

Ears

The shape of your ears also says something about your personality. Soft ears imply sensitivity or that you are listening to your inner and outer worlds. Soft ears like listening to others and they like to study music. Stiff ears may indicate a closed-minded approach to your outer world. They like to rely on their own decisions. Ears that are angled forward specify that you can be easily influenced by others, either positively or negatively. Your ears are vital to your ability to hear how you interpret other people's thoughts and intentions.

The Upper Body

Your upper body (from the waist up) represents your emotional and mental aspects, while your lower body (from the waist down) represents your physicality and sexuality. If your upper body naturally tilts forward, this indicates that you are intellectual, calculating, and visual and that you make decisions based on your old ideas or past experiences. If your upper body naturally tilts backward, you are a "feeling person" and make decisions with your emotions and heart. An upper body that is proportionally bigger than your lower body indicates that you may have a challenge expressing your feelings.

Having a hunched back may indicate that you are carrying a lot of mental and physical responsibility on your shoulders from family, friends, or work; or it may be that you are sitting at a desk under stress for hours at a time. In general, it can indicate that you stress yourself out by helping others. Taking things personally can make you feel mentally and emotionally uncomfortable and unable to keep your mind sharp. Mental, emotional, and spiritual balance is needed especially in your personal life. Socialize and enjoy life with your loved ones and friends.

Breasts and Chest

A naturally elevated chest, breast, or ribcage indicates self-confidence or, in some cases, a big ego. A concave chest shows repression of negative emotions from past love relationships; this can lower your energy. Naturally, large breasts imply the joy of nurturing oneself and others, while small breasts indicate nurturing others before oneself.

Wrists

Large wrists show intellectual aptitude and a love for reading books. Small wrists imply intuitive characteristics and indicates less desire to read books. However, they like being creative. If while a person is lying down the arms are flat and the wrists are facing upward it indicates she/he consciously or unconsciously chooses to react negatively towards others.

Arms

If you keep consciously or unconsciously choosing to cross the left arm over the right arm, it shows some characteristics of right-brain dominance. Crossing the right arm over the left arm implies some left-brain dominance.

Hands

The shape of your hands can reveal some mental characteristics. For instance, when the fingers are close together with the palms open and there are spaces between the knuckles often indicates open-minded and unconventional. However, no spaces between your fingers often indicates idealistic and conventional person. Long fingers may imply that you create and attract opportunities in life without much effort; small fingers indicate that you need to work more than normal to get what you want. Fingers that are bony or skinny may indicate that you are an intuitive person. Large, strong hands show that you have strong willpower to achieve what you desire or want in life. Using this willpower to improve yourself through spirituality is the great gift to possess.

Hugging others with closed fists imply you are mentally and emotionally holding back. Hugging others with your hands open, however, demonstrates that you are mentally and emotionally connected.

Toes

Having long toes may indicate a naturally strong sex drive. Having spaces between your toes implies a strong sexual drive and an inclination to have more than one sexual partner. No spaces between the toes, however, implies that you are sexually faithful to one partner.

Feet

High arches in the feet may indicate that you are a sensitive, emotional person with low self-esteem or that you think a lot. Flat feet implies that you are less emotional and more practical/grounded and make life easy for yourself and others. Walking quickly with your head up indicates that you have high energy and don't like to procrastinate; walking slowly demonstrates that you like to take time doing your personal things. Walking slowly with your head down indicates that you are wondering or worrying about someone or something. Remember, life is always in front of you.

Being pigeon-toed indicates selfishness or an unwillingness to share with people other than your loved ones. Individuals who are standing up or walking with their feet pointing diagonally outwards keep choosing to please others. These people enjoy helping others, and they like to be needed.

Legs

Having bowed legs may implies a strong sex drive. Long legs imply physical stamina and achievement in sports.

Reflexes

Quick reflexes indicate an elevated awareness of the self: your soul, body, and mind work perfectly together. Consciousness can change your physical reality. If you tell yourself out loud every day for several times this affirmation: "I am healthy and strong," "I am patient and tolerant", it can make you healthier. Your body will eventually listen to your command. Believe!

Chapter 29

Our Powerful Brain

Some scientists say we use about ten percent of our brain's capacity. What I believe, however, is that we use about ten percent of the information our soul transfers to our brains. In other words, one of the functions of the brain is to be a filter or a transformer through which we interpret ten percent of the information streaming through our soul's consciousness into our conscious mind.

According to some scientists, there are approximately 100 billion neurons moving around in the brain. I believe that these neurons also represent the soul manifesting itself as consciousness throughout the brain and body. The physical body reflects the mind and soul's consciousness.

I am constantly updating my old belief routine inherited from my ancestors so that I can improve my life. If you keep believing and reminding yourself daily that you are a spiritual being, you will become that person because consciousness can change your physical reality.

Below, I would like to share some of my observations about the brain that may help you to identify yourself:

In the last decades, higher consciousness of our world is illuminating the human's mind; thus we can be more consciously aware of our thoughts, actions, and behaviors. Through this higher consciousness of your soul, you can access your wisdom to overcome your old consciousness, such as the lack of forgiveness, vengefulness, and fearfulness mindset.

In my experience as a professional spiritual life coach for four decades, I have become aware that the first, third, or fifth child is naturally more left-brain dominant, like the father's personality/male energy. Conversely, the second, fourth, or sixth child is naturally more right-brain dominant, like the characteristics of the mother's personality/female energy.

The following are some differences of our right and left-brain characteristics:

Right-Brain Dominant/Female Energy vs Left-Brain Dominant/Male Energy

Second, fourth, sixth child, and so on vs First, third, fifth child, and so on

Action-oriented	Verbal
Ambidextrous	Right-handed
Artistic	Linguistic
Adaptable	Less flexible
Affectionate	Less affectionate
Balance	Busy
Content	Moody
Creative	Copies others
Careless	Perfectionist
Compassionate	Feeling neutral

Dislike rules	Expect rules
Disorganized	Organized
Easy on oneself	Hard on oneself
Extroverted	Introverted
Fearless	Fearful
Feeling	Intellectual
Forgiving	Rancorous
Emotionally detached	Emotionally attached
Goes with the flow	Goes against the flow
Heart thinker	Head thinker
Holistic	Conventional
Live in the moment	Live in the past or future
Leaders	Followers
Lazy	Hard working
Less responsible	Responsible
Non-judgmental	Judgmental
Non-linear	Linear
Passive	Domineering
Optimistic	Pessimistic
Predictable	Unpredictable
Patient	Inpatient
Practical	Calculative
Short-term memory	Long-term memory
Social	Loner
Spontaneous	Planner

Spiritual	Materialistic
Shy	Assertive
Sharing with anyone	Sharing with a few
Trusting/gullible	Suspicious

We can determine whether we are more right-brain or left-brain dominant by highlighting the characteristics in the list above. Being aware of our dominant traits, we can begin to balance our brain characteristics and develop our natural aptitudes and skills including becoming ambidextrous.

Spiritual Definitions

Being a spiritual allows you to experience and attract spiritual words to speak your truth and help others to find theirs.

I briefly define the following terms, which can be used for mindful speech and for realizing your own spiritual journey:

Spirituality

Spirituality is metaphysically evolving into higher consciousness, the grandest freedom and awareness, and the internal experience you are having through your soul. It is the connection to everyone and everything at the energy level within this world and throughout this universe.

As Above, So Below

As above, so below (metaphor) is a spiritual truth and means that whatever exists in heaven (above) at the spiritual or energy level, the abundance of love and compassion, also exists here on Earth (below) at the physical level. This spiritual truth also means that everyone is living life simultaneously in these two different places at the same time.

Beingness

This means being joyfully alive, or passionately driven. It is the highest state of existence of your magnificent soul and Spirit, which creates all circumstances in life. It is in your soul's nature to love yourself and others unconditionally. Through love, you can consciously attract and experience more joy, because joy is love demonstrated.

Heaven

Heaven (our first home) is a spiritual dimension within this physical dimension—right here, right now, where we all reside before joining the physical world (second home) in this galaxy. (Note: By using the word heaven, I am not implying the general concept of "heaven and hell" that some sacred books mention.)

Inner Voice

The inner voice (genderless) is the telepathic voice of your spiritual guide within your soul and sends you messages through your mind and pineal gland. This experience happens in order to encourage you and to keep spiritually evolving.

Love

Love is the grandest and highest state of consciousness/self-awareness and pure energy of the soul and Spirit, which allows you to co-create and evolve spiritually with others. Love allows you to accept, receive, and give the abundance of life to yourself and others unconditionally. When I mention love in this book, I am referring to unconditional love.

Metaphysics

Metaphysics is the cause and effect beyond physical reality. What you are thinking, being, and doing in this present life, whether you are spiritually aware or unaware, will manifest itself on the physical plane. Metaphysicians consciously practice and experience the spiritual laws of the universe in order to evolve **in consciousness** and assist others who are searching for spiritual awareness.

Mind

One of the functions of the mind is to store all your thoughts that accure throughout the body and soul so that you can experience your physical reality. You can also find in your mind your unconditional free will to create your spiritual self-identity, a self-identity that will be different from everyone else.

Nirvana

Nirvana, or paradise, is not a physical or spiritual place waiting for us but is instead the ultimate spiritual awareness and the grandest experience at the energy level of the love within our soul and Spirit. Nirvana is the most profound experience of the highest aspect of love, a place where we can connect with our Creator/Spirit.

Soul

The magnificent and infinite soul is part of the Creator and is an expression of love and compassion of the Spirit at the energy level. This incredible soul is our highest state of consciousness. The soul is also our personal identification with which we can spiritually and physically exists in this universe. When I use the concept of One Soul (we are all One), I am including within this phrase all souls are one in the universe. Your soul's consciousness is your inner self—who you are. Consciousness is spiritual self-awareness or self-reflection of the Spirit.

Ghost

Ghosts or souls are those who have lived here on Earth and have left behind some of the residues of their soul's positive and negative energies. If you are sensitive enough, you can see or hear the pain, the happiness, or suffering left behind at the energy level.

Feelings

Feelings are the language of the soul. Feelings guide you throughout this physical journey so you can evolve spiritually. Your "gut feelings" can be experienced usually in your solar plexus when the soul is communicating with you.

Spirit

Spirit is the extraordinary Creator who resides within our soul and throughout the body, specially in the heart area. The Spirit is the invisible energy that, out of love and through its own energetic self-image, created everyone and everything. Our Creator/Spirit/God doesn't punish nor negatively judge anyone or anything on this planet or in the universe but instead gives us an abundance of love, compassion and wisdom to help us evolve in consciousness.

Third Eye

The third eye is the area of the physical body believed to house a super awareness beyond physical reality. Your third eye is the window of your soul and is located mid-forehead between your eyebrows and is connected to your pineal gland at the center of your brain that facilitate spiritual 360-degree vision and hearing so you can see souls, ghosts and auras of other people at the energy level. The third eye can help you see and find people or things from a very long distance, which is called remote viewing (reading the field's energy or reading people's thoughts).

Your Reality

Your present reality is not what appears to be (what you are seeing) but what you think is happening or what you are seeing in your mind through your old mind's perspective. Your present reality is the accumulation of your opinions, beliefs, behavior, truth, five senses, and subconscious mind, all these things are connected to your past experiences. Everything you see and hear is a perspective and not necessarily the truth. Understanding your spirituality can help you create, see, and experience an ultimate reality that can bring people together in our world. Your spiritual reality is more important than your physical reality because your physical reality most likely hasn't helped you evolve.

Higher consciousness

Higher consciousness (light energy) is the natural state of your soul. It is the state of expressing unconditional love, compassion, joy, peace, wisdom, optimism, and freedom. Moreover, laughter can be a sign of higher consciousness that can make you healthier. Lower consciousness (dark energy), on the other hand is your mind expressing your fears, separation, anxiety, stress, pessimism, anger, greed, control, and lies etc.

Soul Mantra for the Mind

Repeating this prayer-mantra or these affirmations once or twice a day invites your conscious-mind-through your soul-to rise to higher consciousness, to experience Oneness with others. This mantra helps you realize who you truly are. When you start experiencing this mantra through practice, your mind will accept and experience who you really are. Then you can share it with others so they too can remember who they truly are:

Love and Oneness.
I am the light,
I am the Spirit,
I am love,
I am peace,
I am joy,
I am wisdom,
I am freedom,
I am worthy,
There is one family on this Earth,
Our magnificent human family, and
There is one soul on this Earth,
Our magnificent soul.
Amen.

Conclusion

Life is eternal. Life cannot end, because you are one with Spirit, which is life itself. Spirit is forever changing, creating, and recreating itself. You have known this since the beginning of your life. But until now, you will start to awaken your mind. You are eternal.

We are all One! We are all peace! We are all love! Be Love, my Beloved!

Carlos

www.ingramcontent.com/pod-product-compliance
Lightning Source LLC
LaVergne TN
LVHW041224080526
838199LV00083B/2900